Canyon Country Parklands
This first edition belongs to

Name   Date

Water-sculptured sandstone shelters a reflecting pool and a twist of driftwood in the Paria Canyon-Vermilion Cliffs Wilderness Area on the Utah-Arizona border.

CANYON COUNTRY PARKLANDS
Treasures of the Great Plateau

BY SCOTT THYBONY

Prepared by the Book Division
National Geographic Society, Washington, D.C.

CANYON COUNTRY PARKLANDS
Treasures of the Great Plateau

By Scott Thybony

Contributing Photographers: Tom Bean, Miguel Luis Fairbanks,
David Alan Harvey, Dewitt Jones

Published by The National Geographic Society
Gilbert M. Grosvenor, *President and Chairman of the Board*
Michela A. English, *Senior Vice President*

Prepared by The Book Division
William R. Gray, *Vice President and Director*
Margery G. Dunn, Charles Kogod, *Assistant Directors*

Staff for this book
Margaret Sedeen, *Managing Editor*
Greta Arnold, *Illustrations Editor*
Suez B. Kehl, *Art Director*
Victoria Garrett Jones, Melanie Patt-Corner, *Researchers*
Patricia F. Frakes, *Contributing Researcher*
Edward Lanouette, Melanie Patt-Corner, Scott Thybony, Jennifer C. Urquhart,
Picture Legend Writers
Susan M. Carlson, *Map Art*
Carl Mehler, *Map Research*
Sandra F. Lotterman, *Editorial Assistant*
Karen Dufort Sligh, *Illustrations Assistant*

Richard S. Wain, *Production Project Manager*
Lewis R. Bassford, Heather Guwang, H. Robert Morrison, *Production*

Karen F. Edwards, Elizabeth G. Jevons, Artemis S. Lampathakis, Teresita Cóquia Sison,
Marilyn J. Williams, *Staff Assistants*

Manufacturing and Quality Management
George V. White, *Director*
John T. Dunn, *Associate Director*
Vincent P. Ryan, *Manager*
R. Gary Colbert

Jennifer A. Teefy, *Indexer*

A Navajo girl makes an evening run to the east as part of her
kinaalda, *or puberty ceremony. Other rites of the kinaalda include a*
corn-grinding bee, *ritual hair combing and tying, songs, and blessings.*

PRECEDING PAGES: An Easter moon rises above Utah's Padre Bay,
in Lake Powell, part of the Glen Canyon National Recreation Area.

6

GATEWAYS 10

THE HIGH PLATEAUS 38

THE WORLD OF
CANYON COUNTRY
WILDLIFE 66

CANYON HEARTLANDS 82

THE PEOPLE
OF THE
GREAT PLATEAU 126

GRAND CANYON 168

Notes on Photographers
Illustrations Credits   196

Index   197

Acknowledgments
Additional Reading   199

THE NATIONAL PARKS
OF CANYON COUNTRY   200

Shadows creep across the floor
of Monument Valley, on the
Utah-Arizona border. Sandstone
pinnacles, monoliths, and
monument-like buttes such as
East and West Mittens (at left)
gave the name to this region,
which has been a setting for
many Western movies and
television commercials.

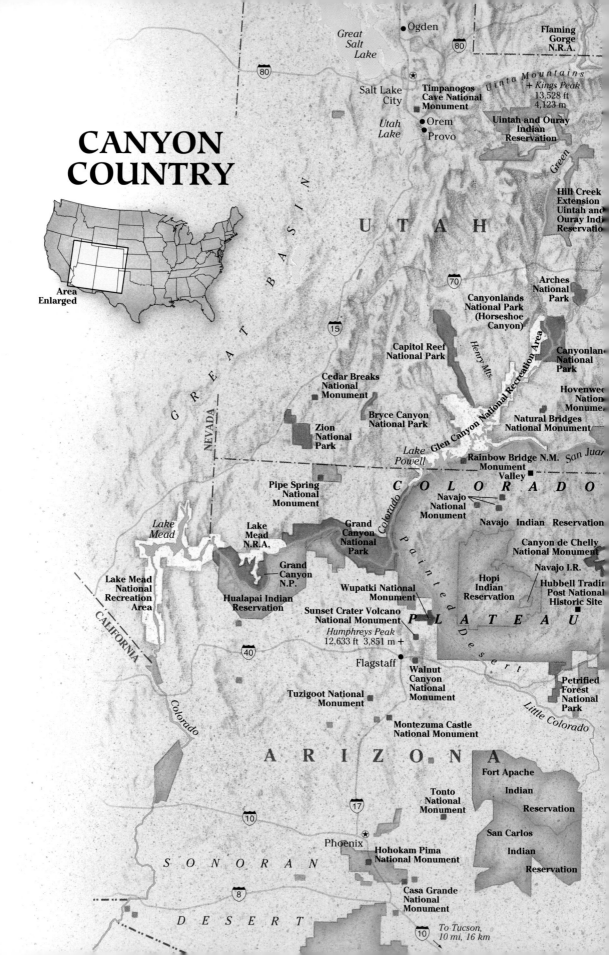

CANYON COUNTRY

Area Enlarged

Great Salt Lake

● Ogden

Flaming Gorge N.R.A.

⊛ Timpanogos Cave National Monument

Salt Lake City

Uinta Mountains

+ *Kings Peak* 13,528 ft 4,123 m

● Orem

Utah Lake

● Provo

Uintah and Ouray Indian Reservation

Green

U T A H

Hill Creek Extension Uintah and Ouray Indi Reservatio

Arches National Park

Canyonlands National Park (Horseshoe Canyon)

Capitol Reef National Park

Henry Mts.

Canyonlan National Park

Cedar Breaks National Monument

Bryce Canyon National Park

Hovenwee Nation Monume.

Natural Bridges National Monument

Zion National Park

Lake Powell

Glen Canyon National Recreation Area

Rainbow Bridge N.M.

San Juar

Monument Valley

C O L O R A D O

Pipe Spring National Monument

Navajo National Monument

Navajo Indian Reservation

Lake Mead

Lake Mead N.R.A.

Grand Canyon National Park

Colorado

Canyon de Chelly National Monument

Navajo I.R.

Grand Canyon N.P.

Painted

Hopi Indian Reservation

Hubbell Tradi Post National Historic Site

Lake Mead National Recreation Area

Hualapai Indian Reservation

Wupatki National Monument

Sunset Crater Volcano National Monument

P L A T E A U

Desert

Humphreys Peak 12,633 ft 3,851 m +

CALIFORNIA

Colorado

Flagstaff

Walnut Canyon National Monument

Petrified Forest National Park

Tuzigoot National Monument

Little Colorado

Montezuma Castle National Monument

A R I Z O N A

Fort Apache

Indian

Reservation

Tonto National Monument

San Carlos

Phoenix ⊛

Hohokam Pima National Monument

Indian

Reservation

S O N O R A N

Casa Grande National Monument

D E S E R T

To Tucson, 10 mi, 16 km

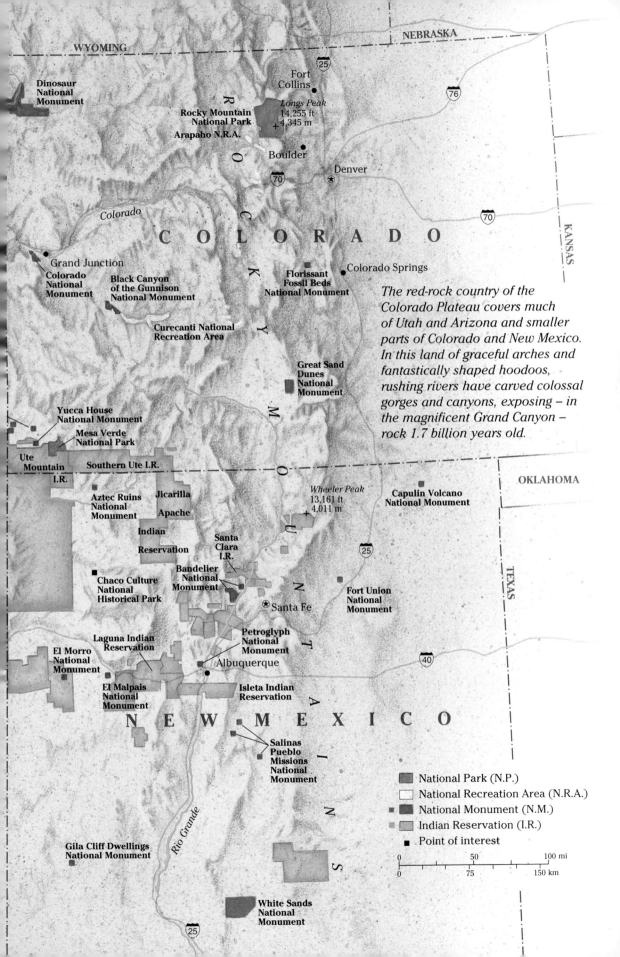

WYOMING

NEBRASKA

Dinosaur National Monument

Fort Collins

Longs Peak 14,255 ft 4,345 m

Rocky Mountain National Park Arapaho N.R.A.

Boulder

Denver

Colorado

C O L O R A D O

KANSAS

Grand Junction

Colorado National Monument

Black Canyon of the Gunnison National Monument

Florissant Fossil Beds National Monument

Colorado Springs

The red-rock country of the Colorado Plateau covers much of Utah and Arizona and smaller parts of Colorado and New Mexico. In this land of graceful arches and fantastically shaped hoodoos, rushing rivers have carved colossal gorges and canyons, exposing – in the magnificent Grand Canyon – rock 1.7 billion years old.

Curecanti National Recreation Area

Great Sand Dunes National Monument

Yucca House National Monument

Mesa Verde National Park

Ute Mountain I.R.

Southern Ute I.R.

OKLAHOMA

Wheeler Peak 13,161 ft 4,011 m

Capulin Volcano National Monument

Aztec Ruins National Monument

Jicarilla

Apache

Indian

Reservation

Santa Clara I.R.

Bandelier National Monument

Chaco Culture National Historical Park

Santa Fe

Fort Union National Monument

TEXAS

Laguna Indian Reservation

Petroglyph National Monument

El Morro National Monument

Albuquerque

El Malpais National Monument

Isleta Indian Reservation

N E W   M E X I C O

Salinas Pueblo Missions National Monument

National Park (N.P.)

National Recreation Area (N.R.A.)

National Monument (N.M.)

Indian Reservation (I.R.)

Point of interest

Gila Cliff Dwellings National Monument

Rio Grande

0   50   100 mi

0   75   150 km

White Sands National Monument

GATEWAYS

Trees of Stone,
Ancient Footprints,
Flowing Corridors of Time

River currents braid together, swinging the bow of the dory toward a breach in the mountain wall before us. On each side of the opening, thick laminations of rock bend skyward in a massive uplift. "The portal," says the boatman as he takes a few strokes forward.

A string of boats threads its way toward the head of Yampa Canyon, past the Vale of Tears and Disappointment Draw. Cliff walls close in as the current increases, drawing the boats down the throat of the gorge, swallowing them in a deep canyon.

Glancing at the map, I trace the line of the Yampa River as it flows west along an arm of Dinosaur National Monument. Joining the Green River, it carves a passage through a spur of the Rocky Mountains to the Colorado Plateau beyond.

The Colorado Plateau is a place where the highest plateaus in North America drop step by step into canyons sunk within canyons. It is a land of standing rocks and painted deserts enclosing one of the greatest concentrations of parklands in the world—nine national parks and dozens of national monuments and wilderness areas. It is a 130,000-square-mile region shaped like the red handprint of an Anasazi pictograph, with the Yampa running along the fingertips, and the corners of four states—Utah, Colorado, New Mexico, and Arizona—meeting at the palm.

This vast maze of canyons and high plateaus was not systematically explored until 1869. In that year Maj. John Wesley Powell led a daring expedition down the Colorado River into the heart of the canyon country. He found more than a blank

PRECEDING PAGES: Nature's handiwork, a convoluted cleft of Navajo sandstone glows with amber hues near Glen Canyon National Recreation Area in Utah. Windblown sand and water have shaped much of the region's landscape.

Framed by willows and ash, Cathedral Rock thrusts spires of sandstone against the Arizona sky near Sedona. Here Oak Creek cuts through pinkish sandstone that gives this part of the plateau its red-rock country nickname.

spot on the map. The soldier-turned-geologist discovered a landscape filled with "strange scenes" and rock forms he did not understand. As the river pulled him deeper into the canyons, he entered what he called "the Great Unknown."

It was winter when I began to travel to the national parks and monuments of the region first mapped by survey parties under Major Powell. I went to see the country at its extremes—Bryce Canyon buried under snow, the Grand Canyon under the glare of a desert sun. I went to find places where the past brushes against the present—like Canyon de Chelly and Chaco Canyon—and places where the land and people connect—such as Canyonlands and Zion. And I went to find what had become of Powell's Great Unknown.

Ahead, the river turns scaly white as it combs across a rock bar. Brad Dimock, top river guide, pushes forward on the oars. His lanky frame bends with each

Dream weaver of the desert, the evening-blooming trumpet flower of the sacred datura adds a grace note to a canyon country landscape. This potent—and poisonous—hallucinogenic plant, also known as thorn apple or jimsonweed, was long used to induce visions during Navajo and Hopi rites. Its fragrance and whitish glow make it attractive to nocturnal moths. Winter floods along the Gunnison River in Colorado (opposite) have left century-old cottonwood trees standing in a polished bed of brittle ice.

stroke as he angles for the deeper channel along the far wall. An inexperienced rower tries to do it all with the arms—pulling too hard and then overcorrecting, fighting the river instead of going with it. Brad reads the water at a glance and gives another well-timed stroke before pausing to let the current take hold of the boat.

I ask him if he's ever had to swim a rapid. "Yes," he says, surprised by the question. "I've swum them all—usually wearing my dory for a hat."

For all their graceful beauty, dories have a drawback—rocks can splinter their wooden hulls. Boatmen run them on the Yampa only when the water is high enough to open a channel through the boulder-strewn gorge. High water is hard to predict on a wild river like the Yampa, the only major tributary of the Colorado River system without a big dam. Its flows change with the seasons and not with the power demands of a distant city. We wanted to catch the crest of the spring runoff, but this year the Yampa peaked earlier than normal because of a warm spring. The volume of water carrying us is only half of what it had been the week before—and falling.

Leaning back on the deck of the boat named *Cataract,* I watch the sky narrow to a band of blue that curves with the river. For a moment, the motion of the boat appears to stop and the band of sky begins to flow. A light wind moves upriver, sounding like the distant rush of white water. A flicker of movement catches my eye as a pair of outstretched wings glides over the rimrock, riding the current of air. "Eagle," Brad says, wearing sunglasses so dark I can't tell where he's looking.

The last time we made a river trip together we were training as boatmen in the Grand Canyon. I left after a few seasons, but Brad remained. The Colorado and its tributaries are in his blood. Of all the white water he has run from Alaska to Chile, he always returns to the great arterial river flowing through the Colorado Plateau. The Green River joins it, then the San Juan, then the Little Colorado. The Colorado

branches across this country, often unseen, lying buried deep within the canyons it has carved.

We soon pull into camp at Anderson Hole—"hole" is a trapper term for a protected pocket in the mountains. Stands of piñon and juniper drop down to the high-water line above where the boatmen fasten their stern lines to metal stakes driven into the beach. Passengers help the crew unload the gear. Once the kitchen is set up, I offer to help, but there's nothing for me to do. The cooks say they'll let me know if they need a hand. Being a passenger is a hard role for me to learn.

That night, at the water's edge, I watch the wild river as it flows west through country unknown to me. Waves lift and sink back upon themselves, endlessly, as the river drags over the rough floor of the canyon. I listen to the water rushing over rock. Spend enough nights on the river and it textures your sleep. A boatman away from the river wakes up at night in a quiet room, listening for a sound that isn't there. The absence of the river leaves a hole in the night.

Next morning we push off as the sun hits the river, turning the dark waters green. I begin to forget the time of day and soon the day of the week. Other rhythms take hold—the daily gathering of storm clouds, the rise and fall of the cliffs as the bedrock uplifts and downwarps. The days become ordered by the making of camp and the breaking of camp, and by the cook's "Come and get it!"

By midmorning on the third day we approach Harding Hole. An island divides the river. The deepest channel runs to the right, chopping across a rock bar and sweeping into an undercut wall. Dodging the shallow rocks, Brad tucks in next to the cliff and rows hard against a strong current that keeps pulling the boat closer and closer to the wall. Streaks of blue paint on the rock mark where others have scraped. With the bow only inches away, we float beneath the overhanging cliff and look up at the bottom of a juniper growing above.

Another dory approaches the riffle, its sides curving upward to a sharply pointed bow with the name *Black Mesa* painted on the side. The current pulls the black dory toward the pale sandstone wall. The bow lifts upward, taking the shape of a cresting wave as the boat shoots past the cliff rock with only inches to spare.

Massive cliffs of light-colored Weber sandstone curve smoothly down toward river level at Harding Hole. Brushing down the smooth walls in delicate traceries that vanish before reaching the bottom is a black fringe of desert varnish—a shiny mineral film on the rock. Spires of dark-green Douglas fir rise at the foot of the white cliff where a young elk breaks from cover. It runs along the top of the talus slope with its head thrown back, then turns into a lateral canyon and disappears.

As the Yampa descends, it trenches into buried geologic layers left by ancient winds and seas, and rivers far older than itself. We float past formations laid down millions of years ago, through a density of time so unimaginable I can grasp it only when it is compressed into the thickness of rock.

We enter classic slickrock country as the river meanders through sandstone corridors divided by spur ridges, sharp-cut and interlocking. In serpentine bends, it loops for seven miles to cover less than two miles on the map. Smooth mural walls lift straight from the river, rounding into domed rimrock high above. Layers thin and flare in cross-sectional profiles of ancient sand dunes cut by the river.

The canyon widens and narrows, the strata dip and rise as the river carves a series of passages through the Uinta Mountains. Each has its own character—distinct yet strangely familiar. It's as if the river practiced here before carving the great canyon parklands to the south. The geology is different, but the form the rock takes is strikingly similar—terraced canyons, palisade walls, slickrock domes.

The underlying geology shapes the character of the landscape. Over millions of years the Colorado Plateau plowed northward, (Continued on page 24)

The Green River makes a hairpin turn around Steamboat Rock, a lofty sandstone monolith overlooking the Echo Park area of Dinosaur National Monument in Colorado. The pea green Yampa joins the Green near the turn.

FOLLOWING PAGES: Desert varnish stripes Tiger Wall on the Yampa River. Moisture has made these markings over the centuries, staining the buff-colored cliff face with glossy residues from dissolved oxides of iron and manganese.

Doryman Bruce Keller scans whitecapped riffles just below S.O.B. Rapid on the Green River at Split Mountain. Close behind, the author's boat, Cataract, *skippered by veteran guide Brad Dimock, plies the channel near a rugged limestone outcropping. At journey's end, river runners (opposite) check hulls for damage as they hoist their dories onto a trailer.*

A Park Service crew coaxes embedded dinosaur remains from a fossil-rich formation at Dinosaur National Monument. Working with a jackhammer, Ron Hopwood (opposite, in brown shirt) enlarges the digging area near a bone so that Rod Joblove and Ann Elder (seated), using hammer and chisel, can expose the fossil and protect it with plaster. Author Scott Thybony (below, foreground) discusses the newly discovered site with Ann and fossil preparator Scott Madsen.

Ancient footprints turned to stone track across the Painted Desert—and tell of teeming life here in moister times. The spore-bearing horsetail plant, a hardy survivor from the age of dinosaurs, still thrives near streams and water holes.

warping the bedrock into the folded and faulted wall of the Uinta Mountains. The plateau itself rests in the eye of a geological storm, squeezed between the dramatic uplift of the Rocky Mountains on one side and the massive faulting of the Great Basin on the other. Instead of buckling, it uplifted en masse. As the plateau rose, its rock layers remained almost flat.

The next day we enter the deepest section of the canyon. Cliff walls stand face to face, plunging more than 1,700 feet from the rim. Just above the rapid we spot a herd of nine bighorn sheep on a ledge high above the river. They pick their way across the rocky track, white rumps flashing as they spring across a deep fissure without hesitation. Once across, a mother pauses to nurse her lamb.

As we float beneath them, a ewe gives a deep-throated bleat that echoes through the narrow canyon. Brad answers with a convincing "baaaaah" of his own that encourages other bighorn to join the conversation. He says he once called to a ram when he was on foot away from the river. The bighorn lowered its head and stomped the ground with one hoof the moment before it charged, chasing him back to the boats where he leaped into the river to escape.

The current slows as the waters back up behind the rapid. In the summer of 1965, a flash flood tore into the river from a side canyon, washing in tons of boulders that formed a new rapid. The same storm loosened a huge slab on the opposite wall that crashed into the river, adding to the debris. It's the one serious rapid on the Yampa; lives have been lost in it.

The boatmen land above Warm Springs to scout the rapid. From a terrace above, they look down on a tangle of rocks and white water. In the middle of the rapid, water pushes over a large boulder and spills down the far side, falling with such velocity it forms a deep hole that can capsize a boat.

But the main concern for wooden dories is the shallow rock bar below. Brad scans it with a pair of binoculars. "It looks very good," he says. "We're happy."

I jump on the *Black Mesa* with two other passengers and boatman Day DeLaHunt, who knows the Dinosaur country well. The boat drifts slowly toward the head of the rapid, bow first, as Day stands up to check our position. He sits back and takes a few strokes to shift the angle of the boat. The dory slides down the smooth tongue, accelerating as it plunges into the churning water below. The boat dips and jumps with the break of the waves.

Using a minimum of strokes, Day cuts right as the dory slides past the big hole. Pulling left, he straightens the bow, heading for the shallows below. He rows against the current to slow the boat's forward momentum. The boatman picks his way through the rock pile and into the smooth water below without a nick.

The next morning we reach the confluence with the Green River. At this point the Yampa flows gently from east to west, meeting the south-flowing Green at a right angle against the smooth face of Steamboat Rock. As we drift along, Brad gives a long blow on a conch shell. "HOOO-OOOO, Hooo-ooo, hooo-ooo," the notes echo hauntingly between the canyon walls. As the sound trails off, we float in silence past a human-shaped petroglyph weathered faceless on the cliff wall above us.

Major Powell made his camp on the far bank during the 1869 and 1871 expeditions. He named it Echo Park. Conservationists in the 1950s successfully fought a proposed dam that would have flooded Lodore Canyon on the Green and Yampa Canyon, and buried Echo Park under 500 feet of water.

Rounding the bend, we enter the billion-year-old Precambrian rocks of Whirlpool Canyon and make our last camp at the mouth of Jones Hole Creek. Most of the passengers and crew take a hike up the creek, skirting cascading waters and the thick riparian growth. About two miles above camp, we reach a rock overhang the archaeologists call Deluge Shelter. Artifacts retrieved from it indicate that Indians have been passing through the area for the past 7,000 years.

Three square-headed figures, painted in bloodred pigments, stand shoulder to shoulder on the wall above us. Lines radiating from their heads may represent headdresses. The designs resemble an almost perfectly preserved headdress found cached in a Yampa Canyon cave. Centuries ago, Fremont Indians attached 350 black-and-orange flicker feathers to this headband and trimmed it with ermine.

"Holy mackerel," Brad says as he walks up and spots the pictographs. "Those hairstyles look like mine."

After a few days on the river, his hair gets a little prickly, his blond mustache more untamed, and his choice of wardrobe wilder. He began the trip in grays and blues. But that night at the campfire, wearing baggy India print pants and a bright plaid shirt, he tells a round of river stories more animated than any yet. When the tales end, he climbs on his boat and stretches across the hatches to sleep.

As the sky lightens the next morning, Day DeLaHunt begins to get breakfast together. He throws a few fistfuls of coffee grounds into a black enamel pot and sets it on the fire to boil. About this time Brad sits up wrapped in a sleeping bag, watching the water flow past his boat, mesmerized by the river.

By noon we're passing through Rainbow Park under a hot sun. A lone merganser lies slumped across a river cobble, looking more like a beanbag than a duck; on the other bank, a blue heron stands stiff-legged. As we approach, it spreads its long, smoke blue wings and lifts above the rocks. The placid river heads for a dip on the horizon straight ahead, channeling through the softer deposits. But suddenly it swings left, aiming directly into the hard rock mass of Split Mountain.

Geological events often lie hidden, buried beneath the surface. But all is exposed at Split Mountain, and nothing makes sense. The river turns out of its logical course and cuts straight through a mountain instead of around it.

Powell thought the river had established its course before the formation of the mountain, but geologists now believe the mountain came first. A recent theory holds that the Green River cut its present course across the surface of sediments that had buried the preexisting mountain. The river continued to grind downward in its set course as the overlying sediments eroded, uncovering the buried mountain.

The erosion uncovered remnants of an ancient environment. A formation known as the Morrison outcrops along the base of Split Mountain, with sandstone beds deposited by rivers 145 million years ago. Within these rocks lies one of the world's richest concentrations of fossil dinosaur bones.

Before descending the last few miles of our trip on the Green River, we stop for lunch. I sit in the shade facing the river, letting the moment stretch. Behind the moving water the canyon walls rise still and timeless. Where I see a cliff, blank and featureless under a straight-up sun, a geologist reads a story of change—seas covering the land and receding again and again, mountains rising and tumbling, rivers braiding across low coastal plains long before this landmass uplifted into a high desert. A geologist looks at a rock and sees more than a rock.

Earlier, on the way to the put-in on the Yampa, driver Frank McKnight had told us he once shuttled a group of river runners to Rainbow Park on a day when his brakes weren't working too well. "I told one of the passengers to put a rock behind the rear wheel to keep us from rolling back," he said.

The passenger picked up what he thought was a rock, but Frank recognized it at once. He had spent three years at Dinosaur chiseling bones from the wall at the visitor center. The man held a large fragment of a dinosaur femur in his arms. "Lay that thing down very carefully," Frank said, "and get me a *rock.*"

Before the river trip, the park's paleontologist, Dan Chure, had me look at a rock. I met him in his office at the Dinosaur Quarry, discovered in 1909 when a scientist noticed eight fossil tailbones weathering from the rock. The site became a national monument six years later, but not before museum crews had removed 350 tons of dinosaur bones. Park rangers left the remaining fossils in place, exposing more than 2,000 bones in high relief on a vertical rock slab.

Dan sat before a computer screen with a cast of dinosaur tracks on one side and a herd of inflatable toy dinosaurs on the other. Changing desks, he placed a chunk of greenish mudstone under a microscope and had me take a look. A string of delicate bones as fine as the veins of a leaf came into focus. The paleontologist filled me in as I studied them. "It's an embryo," he said. "They're very rare."

This was the first dinosaur embryo found in the park, he added, and one of only a few reported for the entire Morrison. Dan called it a *Camptosaurus,* a plant-eating dinosaur that grew in adulthood up to 20 feet long. This one, he said, never grew longer than 9 inches.

Park Service fossil preparator Scott Madsen walked into the office. He had spent two months preparing the embryo specimen, using only a carbide needle to uncover the delicate bones. The last time I had seen Scott was on a trip to the

Painted Desert to look for fossils. Now he was ready to take me into the field where they were excavating a new dinosaur—with chisels and jackhammers this time.

We drove close to the site, then walked up a draw that led through the faded blue and red bands of the Morrison formation. Above us, a crew of three worked on the side of a sandstone wedge that tilted upward at a sharp 70-degree angle.

After climbing to the site, Scott introduced me to fossil preparator Ann Elder, who knelt next to a large bone embedded in the rock. The reddish black of the fossil contrasted with the pale yellow of the surrounding matrix. Ann and Scott, helped by two volunteers, had exposed the back half of a 25-foot-long dinosaur, and the bones continued into the rock with no end in sight. No one knew how deep beneath the surface they went.

Crew member Rod Joblove rested his heavy tools for a moment. The retired aerospace engineer said he had been on his way back from Canada last year when he stopped at the park to volunteer for a month. He got hooked, stayed for six months, and returned again this year. "It gives you one hell of an appreciation," he said with a smile, "for what someone goes through before a dinosaur gets mounted."

Ann carefully chiseled around a femur, removing the channel sands deposited by a river that had buried the meat-eater long ago. The dinosaur skeleton remained in the flexed position it had taken after death. Finding a carnivore is rare, Dan Chure had told me, and it's even rarer to find an articulated skeleton, especially in the lower Morrison. Even more surprising, I thought, is a discovery occurring so close to the quarry, one of the most visited and most studied dinosaur sites in the world. But luck plays its role in fossil hunting, as I had learned in the Painted Desert.

The Painted Desert runs southeast from the Grand Canyon in a sweeping arc along the Little Colorado River to Petrified Forest National Park. It's a land of stark beauty where sand dunes climb wind-carved cliffs and petrified wood spills from hills banded in multiple hues. Early in the spring I spent a night at the national park camped in a place called the Black Forest. There wasn't a tree in sight.

In the morning I rolled against something hard. Opening my eyes, I saw a log of dark petrified wood. Other logs, in cordwood-size segments, lay scattered about where they had tumbled from the eroded hummocks above. Sitting up, I looked down Lithodendron Wash and across the Painted Desert badlands, barren of all but a few stone trees working their way to the surface after more than 200 million years.

Farther south in the park, petrified wood weathers from the Chinle Hills in pockets of beautifully fossilized logs colored in vivid hues of red, yellow, and occasionally blue. Detail is so well preserved in some that insect tunnels and lightning scars can be seen—but not bark or limbs. Floodwaters stripped these from the tall conifers as they were carried long distances before being covered by mud and volcanic ash. Mineral-rich water saturated the wood and over time replaced the organic tissue with quartz. Rivers at Petrified Forest buried the trees 80 million years earlier than the rivers at Dinosaur had buried the carcasses of the giant reptiles.

Leaving the Black Forest camp, I walked through the banded pastels of the Chinle formation to Kachina Point. The Painted Desert Inn, restored by the Park Service as a museum, stood on the rim. Inside, wearing a traditional full satin skirt, a Navajo weaver sat before her loom. Wool yarn wrapped her gray hair. "The pattern comes from inside," said Mary Ann Morris as she wove rich red yarns into the design of her rug. "All the time I pray as I go along. I pray as I weave." A shank of yarn lay in her lap. She called the color Ganado red. "It's the color in those petrified woods," she said, motioning toward the badlands outside the window, "out in the desert."

I first went to the Painted Desert country, north of Petrified Forest, after telling my young son Erik that I would locate a dinosaur bone for him to see. It was one of those rash promises a father sometimes makes and immediately regrets. Never having seen a dinosaur bone in the wild before, I had no idea of where to begin looking. But I asked around and soon narrowed the search area to a 200-square-mile piece of the Painted Desert that would take a lifetime to cover.

After several unsuccessful trips, I returned with Scott Milzer, a friend who wanted to spend a few days in the desert before joining his fishing boat off Alaska. Leaving a dirt road that followed the Little Colorado River, we turned onto a track leading up a dry wash toward a break in the cliffs. The faint trace quickly disappeared, washed clean by recent rains.

Topping the first escarpment beyond the river, we faced a line of deep-red cliffs rising from a field of sand dunes. Most of the sand had weathered from the higher cliffs of Navajo sandstone, itself an ancient dune field. Milzer put on his rose-colored sunglasses to get the full effect. We could see for miles across a treeless expanse without a piece of wood in sight—petrified or otherwise.

Leaving the truck behind, we set out on foot to find a set of dinosaur tracks that Scott Madsen had rediscovered a few months before. The legendary Barnum Brown first recorded them in 1929. Brown was an adventure-prone paleontologist who hunted fossil bones throughout the world for the American Museum of Natural History. On one expedition he fell into an extinct volcano; on another he was shipwrecked and marooned south of Tierra del Fuego.

Brown led an expedition to the Painted Desert and found what turned out to be one of the largest dinosaur trackways in the Southwest. He located nearly 300 tracks—some left by a dinosaur the size of a turkey, others by one estimated to be 25 feet long. Over the years Brown's field notes disappeared, and sand drifted over the site. Geologists knew only its general location when Madsen decided to look for it. He carried with him an old photograph of the track site and walked over the area until the skyline in the photo matched the one in the field. Then, clearing away sand at the most likely spot, he found the lost trackway.

As Milzer and I hiked in the general direction of the tracks, we could see a lone spire of red rock topping a distant rise. I mentioned that Barnum Brown had carved his name in the base of it, but by then Milzer was skeptical of the whole trackway story. He said he didn't trust anybody with the name of Barnum.

I expected to take most of the morning searching for the tracks, but we got lucky. A pocket of red hoodoos enclosed the site, once on the dune-bordered shore of a Triassic sea. We followed one set of three-toed prints, with claw marks clearly visible, for several strides until they disappeared beneath a slip of sand. Runoff from a recent storm had washed over the site, burying many of the others.

We left the site, spreading out as we circled back to the truck on the chance we might spot new tracks. As I crossed a shallow wash, I noticed a few pieces of bluish rock unlike the surrounding sandstone. I stopped to take a closer look. The rock had the grainy texture of a worked-over dog bone. It had to be fossilized bone.

Madsen had told me that fossils were rare in the Moenave sandstone, so I followed the pieces of bone as they trailed up the dry wash to an isolated butte. Rib fragments and vertebrae littered the ground beneath a red sandstone cliff; other bones weathered from the bedrock itself. The only known fossils from this formation are an early form of crocodile called a *Protosuchus* and some fish scales. This was different—something I hoped might let me keep my promise. Marking the find on the map, we returned to town.

The next week, I went back to the site with Madsen and my son. Scott wanted to be sure the bone came from the Moenave formation. We drove as close to the site as possible, then hiked the last half mile. When Scott saw the bluish-white bone actually embedded in the Moenave rock, he was convinced. "This is amazing!" he kept saying. "I can't believe it. This is great!"

He guessed that the bones came from a small carnivore, perhaps a new species of dinosaur, the first ever reported from this formation. Brushing away a layer of dirt, he exposed a few ankle bones. The temptation to keep digging was strong, but he restrained himself. Excavation has to be done right or the specimen can be ruined. The dinosaur would have to wait.

Erik spent the time on his hands and knees crawling along the wash searching for bone fragments. Suddenly he stood up, throwing his arms in the air. "I wouldn't want to be anywhere else in the whole world," he said.

I step out of the shade next to the Green River at the head of Split Mountain Canyon. Lunch is over and it's time to head downriver. Pushing the boat into the current, I step aboard.

The Green races into the gorge, slicing a cross section through the flared walls, layered like the rings of a petrified log. It drops a fast 20 feet per mile through four boulder-choked rapids. Waves slap across the gunwales as the boats buck through the sharp-pitched waves. Each rapid gives an exhilarating ride, but not a single dory makes it through Split Mountain unscathed. Each hull gives a hollow clunk as it glances off an unseen rock.

Nearing the outlet, the current slackens. Our trip draws to a close, but the river keeps flowing south. The Green River meanders through the last folds of Split Mountain as the white cliffs fall away. For a moment, the canyon walls frame the Colorado Plateau country, stretching like a painted canvas before us, the river a single brush stroke leading into it.

Humanlike figures and animals adorn Deluge Shelter, a rock overhang in Dinosaur National Monument that has served as a temporary campsite for some 7,000 years. Prehistoric Indians known as Fremont people (for the river where their culture was first identified) created these pictographs between A.D. 200 and 1250, using as paint iron oxides mixed with animal fat.

FOLLOWING PAGES: Using a different technique, Indian artisans chiseled and chipped through rock coated with dark desert varnish to create this petroglyph panel in the Painted Desert.

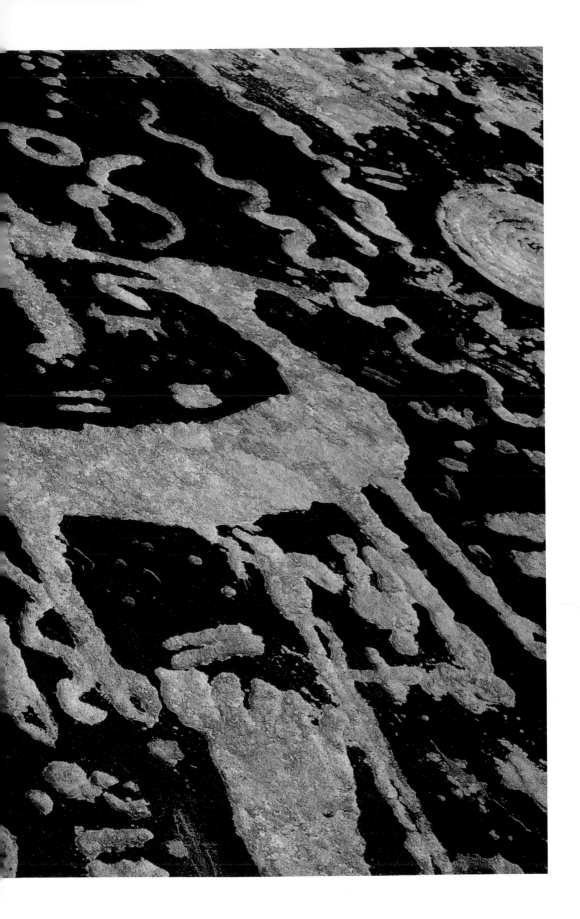

Logs turned to stone lie in Arizona's Petrified Forest National Park. The trees, long-extinct kinds of conifers, grew 200 million years ago. Eventually they toppled into streams and lost bark and boughs before coming to rest on a floodplain. Sediments buried the stranded trunks, and waterborne minerals filled interstices (below), replacing the wood. The land rose about 65 million years ago, and erosion has been stripping away the overburden ever since, gradually exposing the logs.

Sandstone cross-beds make a billowing staircase for a hiker in the Paria Canyon-Vermilion Cliffs Wilderness Area of southern Utah. The canyon is so remote that a 200-foot-high arch nearby was unknown to the outside world until the 1960s. Pressure over time forced sandstone layers (above) into swirls.

FOLLOWING PAGES: Mounds below the Vermilion Cliffs display banded hues also common to the Painted Desert. Iron oxides impart reddish tints; decayed, unoxidized vegetation creates bluish tones.

THE HIGH
PLATEAUS

Hoodoos, Temples, and Towers Wrought by Wind and Water

S now falls on the rim of Bryce Canyon. It has been falling on and off for weeks as storms trail across the high country of southern Utah. Snow is falling on the Markagunt Plateau to the west, cut by Zion Canyon and Cedar Breaks. It is falling to the east on the cloud-hidden Aquarius, the highest plateau in North America. And it is falling here on the Paunsaugunt Plateau.

Leaving the ski trail behind, I cross an untracked slope to a sheltered grove above the cliffs of Bryce Canyon. I ease the heavy pack to the ground and find a place to make camp for the night. Digging a snow trench large enough to pitch a tent takes half an hour. Pegs won't hold in the fine powder, so I use the ski poles as anchors. Simple things like tying a knot take longer in the cold; stiff fingers force me to think through each step. By the time the tent is up, the winter night has settled among the trees. I crawl inside as the snow continues to fall.

A couple of days before, I had left my home in Arizona and followed the highway into the Painted Desert and across the Colorado River. Beyond the river, the highway ascended a stairway of cliff-walled terraces, climbing north from the Grand Canyon to the highest plateaus. Barrier cliffs, named for their distinct colors—the Vermilion, the White, and the Pink—formed each step. As pickup trucks passed, I tried to guess where they had been from the color of the mud splattered on their fenders. Lots of vermilion rumbled by, but few came from the higher country where snow drifts still blocked the back roads.

PRECEDING PAGES: A cloud-swept sky beams a sunny spotlight on the West Temple in Utah's Zion National Park. Rising some 3,800 feet above the canyon floor, the sandstone buttress wears a tree-fringed cap, a vestige of an ancient dune.

Rainbowed showcase of sculptured stone, Utah's Cedar Breaks National Monument has been carved into a 2,000-foot-deep amphitheater of spires, columns, arches, and canyons by runoff rivulets gnawing at the lip of the Markagunt Plateau.

The highway topped the shoulder of the Paunsaugunt Plateau and ran beneath a low cloud ceiling moving eastward. Banks of plowed snow lined the road as it crossed the white expanse to the hoodoo valleys of Bryce Canyon National Park.

Just before the entrance station to Fairyland Point I put on my skis, anxious to see the park for the first time in winter. A cross-country ski trail followed an unplowed spur road leading to the rim. Well packed by skiers, the trail ran straight and level through a corridor of ponderosa pines so snow-shrouded that only the undersides of the branches showed.

I soon caught up with a family of eight, shuffling along in single file on skis

rented from a nearby lodge. Those at the front talked excitedly, thrilled to be skiing for the first time; the others were silent, concentrating on each tentative step. Suddenly, the woman bringing up the rear gave a shriek as her feet took off without the rest of her, sending her into a snowbank for a soft landing. As her daughter helped her up, both laughed at the size of the sitzmark pressed into the snow.

Trees thinned as the trail climbed the rim crest. The sky expanded, giving a sense of open space beyond. As I reached the edge of the plateau, the sun broke through a rift in the clouds, transforming the snow into pure light. An infusion of red and orange flooded the maze of interlocking ravines separated by knobby fins and fluted walls. I planted my skis next to the drop and stared at the intricately carved limestone, saturated with colors so luminous they seemed unreal.

Strangely weathered rock pillars called hoodoos crowded the interior slopes. To Paiute Indians, hoodoos were the remnants of the Legend People, animals that had the power to appear in human form. Trickster-hero Coyote turned the creatures into stone when they defied him after he invited them to live in the village he had built for them in the cliffs. According to the Indians, Coyote always does the opposite of what he is told—a trait shared by humans since he was the one who taught people how to live. "His tracks are still there in the earth," said a Paiute elder, "and we step in them as we walk."

To a geologist, hoodoos are erosional remnants. Massive faulting has exposed the Pink Cliffs and the softer, underlying shales to the rapid downcutting of melting snows and fierce thunderstorms. Rain carves the rock, runoff gouges it, and meltwater refreezes and splits it. The weathering edge of the plateau recedes from about one and a half feet to as much as four feet each century.

At that rate of erosion, Mormon pioneer Joseph Fish had to walk a step or two farther to reach the rim than I did. In 1866 he led an exploring party across the plateau, struggling through heavy rains and fearing attack by Indians. "This range of mountains presented almost a perpendicular wall almost as far as the eye could reach," he wrote in one of the first recorded descriptions of the Bryce country.

A few years later, John Wesley Powell reached the summit of the plateau. A

Weathered sandstone and limestone (opposite) call to mind a mad organist's pipe dream in Utah's Bryce Canyon National Park, a pocket gouged in the Paunsaugunt Plateau by marauding water. "A helluva place to lose a cow," complained pioneer Ebenezer Bryce. A bristlecone pine (right) clings to life near a castle-like formation. Among earth's oldest living things, such trees at Bryce have survived up to 1,600 years.

sea of clouds gathered below him, scaling the cliffs as he watched and enclosing the rim in a thick mist. Searching for a lost mule, Powell climbed what he thought was a low ridge and looked out. At that moment the wind stirred, parting the clouds below and revealing "an almost bottomless abyss" that fell at least 2,000 feet.

Mormons began to settle along the foot of the plateau less than five years after Powell's climb. In 1875 Ebenezer Bryce built a cabin near the mouth of a drainage his neighbors called Bryce's Canyon. He moved away five years later, but others took his place, founding the town of Tropic.

At first glance, Tropic in winter looks bleak. Barren hills enclose a town of 600 residents. The main two-lane highway through town crosses the dry bed of Bryce Creek and skirts the dry bed of the Paria River. Stubbly fields lie dormant, backyard orchards stand bare-limbed. But the warmth of the local residents doesn't depend on the season.

I turn onto a side street that becomes a dirt road not far beyond the house of Wallace Ott, cattleman and former county commissioner. He welcomed me at his door wearing a plaid shirt, Levi's, *(Continued on page 50)*

FOLLOWING PAGES: Thor's Hammer, an eroded rock column called a hoodoo, greets the dawn of a new day at Bryce. Paiute Indian legend holds that such formations throughout the park were evildoers turned to stone by an angry god.

A cross-country skier takes the low road
along the Navajo Loop Trail in Bryce
Canyon, squeezing between 200-foot-
high sandstone cliffs laid down as lake-
bottom sediments some 60 million years
ago. Over time, the land has slowly
thrust upward more than a mile, baring
these rocks to water's cutting flow.
Encompassed by walls of rock, Douglas
firs (above) reach for the sky. These
700-year-old giants survive by sinking
taproots deep into the ground.

FOLLOWING PAGES: Sunrise ignites
the battlements of a Bryce Canyon
formation. Water and ice wearing away
at rock layers of varying hardness have
shaped this enchanted place.

and polished boots. Born in this country 80 years ago, he rides a horse almost every day to tend a herd of cows kept south of town. Inside he began telling a story about a former neighbor, Lige Moore, who always wore a ten-gallon Stetson and carried his false teeth in a pouch tied behind his saddle. Lige and his sons spent most of their time tending cattle down on the range, Wallace said. "One night, one of the boys asked how he could eat beef without his teeth. 'Well boys, that's easy. I just put a piece in my mouth, gum it around until it gets dizzy, and then I swallow it.' "

Lige once invited Wallace to his place to meet an old friend—a man named Butch Cassidy. Wallace spent the morning listening to the tales of the man who claimed to be the famous outlaw, long after newspapers had reported his death. Cassidy had grown up in a town not far away and once danced with Wallace's mother. He told Wallace he first got into trouble with the law after getting into a fight at a dance and breaking a man's jaw. Early the next morning Cassidy fled across the plateau pursued by the sheriff.

"Ol' Butch could hear the posse a-gaining on him," Wallace said. "He could hear their horses' hooves hitting the rocks in the creek bottom." The lawmen thought they had Butch cornered below Tropic, but he gave them the slip and headed up the side of the Paunsaugunt, mixing his horse's tracks with those from a band of wild horses. He then hid in an old cabin built by Wallace's grandfather. Soon Cassidy escaped across the Bryce badlands to the rim country above. "He stole from the rich and gave to the poor," Wallace added. "And he never stole any cattle."

L eaving Fairyland Point, I skied south along a trail that hugged the edge of the plateau. Ski tracks pointed in the direction of Bryce Point about four miles away. I pushed along with a kick-glide, kick-glide motion until a ski tip angled out of the track and caught in the softer snow. Then it was flounder, plod-tromp, plod-tromp until I found the trail again.

Wind and recent snowfall had obliterated most of the old track, making it hard to stay on course. I began breaking trail through deep powder—plowing through drifts waist high and avoiding clumps of buried manzanita. A few red limbs, stippled with leaves that stay green all winter, poked through the snow cover. The exposed limbs may die during a long cold spell, but an insulating layer of snow protects most of the bush from the bitter cold.

After switchbacking up a steep promontory, I stopped for a moment on top. Everywhere I looked, snow softened the landscape. Erosion had worked the Paunsaugunt into a serrated edge of amphitheaters and alcoves. The largest amphitheater, about three miles long and two across, is labeled Bryce Canyon on the map, but it resembles a deep pocket cut into the face of the escarpment more than a canyon. The first time I saw Bryce I had a vague feeling that something was missing until I realized it's a canyon with only one side.

The wind shredded the clouds in a pattern matching the ragged edge of the plateau. To the north, the prow of the Sinking Ship tilted skyward, the only rock mass out of kilter in these level benchlands. A snow cloud hung above the 11,000-foot summit of the Aquarius Plateau in the distance. Below, ravines slashed into the flanks of the plateau, exposing the paint-red cliffs—the same rock outcropping on the face of the Aquarius. With a shift of light, it turned shades of orange and pink.

A geologist can look at the unmoving limestone layers of Bryce Canyon and see the quiet accumulation of sediments on a lake bottom, waves crashing on an ancient shore, rivers emptying into lakes. A geologist pays attention to unseen forces still at work—the buckling and splitting of rock masses, the uplift of plateaus, and the transformation of bone and shell into stone.

Jeff Eaton, a geologist-paleontologist with the Museum of Northern Arizona, often watches the colors shift on the face of the Aquarius from the porch of his adobe house in Tropic. He has spent years in southern Utah studying the rocks and searching for fossils. Jeff's house became a field station last year for a museum crew collecting fossils from a layer below the Pink Cliffs. Each day they hiked down the steep switchbacks beneath the rim, bagged their finds, and lugged them back up the trail. The hard work paid off. Upon washing the samples, they discovered the fossil tooth of an early marsupial—the first mammal fossil found in the park.

I asked Jeff to fill me in on the local geology as he installed a wood stove in his house. I was curious about the Claron formation of the Pink Cliffs. It can be seen in the palisades of Table Cliff on the Aquarius, the hoodoo valleys of Bryce, and the eroded escarpment at Cedar Breaks National Monument.

Lake-deposited limestones more than 50 million years old make up most of the rock, Jeff said. In places he has found the fossil shells of freshwater mollusks, including wave-tossed fragments from the ancient lakeshore.

Jeff took a break from his work. We stepped outside the house and looked up at the Paunsaugunt. Bryce Point rose dramatically a few miles away and 2,000 feet higher than where we stood. He said his young daughter noticed the cliffs when she sat in a swing next to the house. "She called them 'beautiful rocks.' And she's right," he added, looking up at the vivid geologic exposures. "They are beautiful."

At the park visitor center, I got a backcountry permit to camp on the rim. Originally, I had intended to snowshoe into Bryce Canyon and spend the night below, but the rangers had closed the trails. Forecasters warned of extreme avalanche danger—a condition rare in southern Utah, but one taken seriously. The day before, four skiers had died in an avalanche in the La Sal Mountains near Moab, Utah.

Deep snows push most of the larger mammals, such as elk and mule deer, into the lower reaches. But many of the smaller animals burrow beneath the ground, waiting for milder weather. A day or two earlier, park ranger Edd Franz told me, a weasel had left its den to search for food. To survive in winter, weasels grow white coats that blend with the surroundings. "This one was dragging a jackrabbit twice its size across the snow," Edd said.

Like the elk, most humans have retreated to the lower country by early November. Even so, during the following six months the park receives some 15 percent of its yearly visitation. Winter in the high plateaus is a time for solitude, unlike summer when more than a million visitors reach the most accessible viewpoints. "They may leave nothing but footprints," Susan Colclazer, chief of interpretation, told me, "but there are places on the rim that get such heavy use you want to say don't even leave those."

In the pre-dawn dark, I roll over and look outside the tent to check the weather. Newly fallen snow covers my tracks, but the storm has passed and the clouds have disappeared. A night sky of deep cobalt blue spreads above the trees, so clear there's no grain to the darkness. The field of snow below gathers light from the moon, turning the surface a lunar white.

The sky has lightened a shade or two by the time I've shed the sleeping bag and clamped the skis to my frozen boots—the ones I neglected to take with me into the sleeping bag. A streak of gray light, dimmer than the moon, spreads along the eastern horizon where the sun will rise. The planet Jupiter shines like a star in the west, still bright enough to be seen on the edge of day.

Weaving among snow-buried trees, I ski a few hundred feet to a crest of rock that screens what lies below the rim. Snow drapes the outcropping rock like an extra geological layer. I spread the ski tips to keep from sliding back and climb with a herringbone step toward a notch flanked by hoodoos standing spectral white. Early geologists used architectural terms to describe these rock forms—ruined colonnades, minarets, turrets. But these have weathered into nameless shapes that existed long before architect or geologist.

With each step up the snow-covered ridge, the world beyond the rim sinks downward. A line of cliffs appears below, its red walls beginning to soak through the night blue. They curve in an amphitheater that collects the headwaters of Yellow Creek. Another step up, and a deep vista opens beyond.

The clarity of the air pulls in the far horizon, giving a sharp edge to the distance. Looking across a land of mesas and canyons, I recognize Navajo Mountain—a blue mound lifting above the skyline 90 miles to the southeast. Lying roughly at the center of the Colorado Plateau, the mountain is holy to the Navajo. They call it Naatsis'áán, "head of earth woman." Standing there, I remember a story Wallace Ott told about the first time he saw Bryce Canyon, before the park existed. "I thought it was pretty," he said, "but I didn't think it was so special, I guess." He paused a moment, remembering himself as a young cowboy on horseback, looking into the colorful badlands below. He was six years old. "I never been anywhere then—I was raised on a ranch just underneath. I thought there was Bryce Canyons all over the world."

Pale sunlight, filtered by a line of low clouds, washes across the face of the plateau. The wind sweeps the fine, dry snow before it as I turn away from the rim.

Two weeks later, morning light floods the cliffs of Zion National Park as I walk with two friends up a slickrock ridge. Above us, on the East Rim of Zion Canyon, Deertrap Mountain tapers to a summit as flat as an altar, hiding the Great White Throne behind it. Deertrap is not really a mountain or a mesa but a conical tower rising as abruptly as a mountain, capped as flat as a mesa, and cut, on one side, as sheer as a canyon wall.

Studying the summit from below, I don't see an obvious route leading to it. The lower slopes can be friction climbed, keeping the feet in maximum contact with the rock and hands pressed flat on the steeper pitches. But no matter how we approach the sheer upper cliffs, we will need a route with handholds and toeholds.

"Sometimes it looks oversteep," Bob Dye says, "but then there'll be a micro-ledge that will let you get up." He talks from beneath a blue baseball cap pulled low against a pair of sunglasses. A full beard covers the rest of his face—good protection from the sunlight. He spends much of his time exploring the canyon country when he's not guiding river trips.

"You can't tell from a distance," Tony Williams adds. Tony wears a canvas

No lonesome cowboy, he. Each season, from about March into November, Chris Jacobs and a handful of other trail riders guide hundreds of visitors along Zion's horse trails. Outings last from a few hours to all day long.

hat and, like Bob, sunglasses and a beard. I stand between them, hatless and whiskerless, listening. Both are old Zion hands who have crisscrossed much of the park's backcountry. "Small increments in slope will make all the difference," Tony continues. "If you keep your weight over your feet, it's amazing what you can go up."

Earlier that morning Bob and Tony suggested we scrap our original plans to hike directly across the plateau to Echo Canyon and take what Tony called "a more interesting route." It meant climbing Deertrap Mountain first and then crossing to Echo Canyon, ending at Weeping Rock on the floor of Zion Canyon about 12 miles away. I readily agreed, although I was unfamiliar with the route. The weather was mild, and I had been told that most of the snow had melted.

But snow still clings to the hollows at the foot of the mountain, piled against drifts of sand turned to stone. In every direction, Navajo sandstone surrounds us, the walls etched in the graceful curves of ancient sand dunes. The rock holds the shape of winds that blew for millions of years across a vast Mesozoic landscape stretching from Wyoming to Arizona. The winds swept grains of almost pure quartz into dunes, eventually gathering into deposits up to 2,200 feet thick.

Navajo sandstone creates a landscape of rare beauty wherever it outcrops. Flowing water carves the rock into slot canyons, deep alcoves, and massive palisade walls. Exposed as rimrock, the sandstone weathers into slickrock domes and undulating dune fields of solid rock that no wind has shifted for 200 million years.

The sandstone cliffs around us drain of color as they lift upward, the last of the reds fading into a wall of white rock. The color range of the Navajo, from deep

Desert pothole, carved by water swirling stones in a fracture, or declivity, dimples a sandstone slope at Zion. Such pools at times hold thriving microcosmic communities of life—fleas, gnats, mosquitoes, snails, even frogs and fairy shrimp.

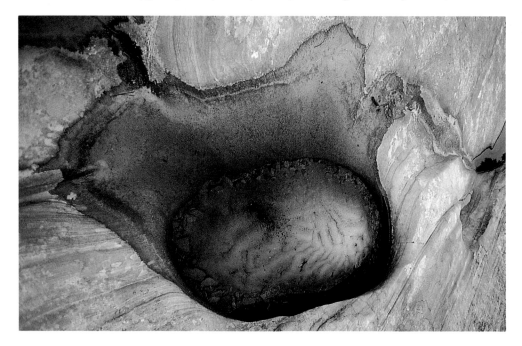

reds to almost pure white, depends on the "bleaching" action of groundwater over millions of years and on the amount of iron oxides present. After deposition, the oxides leached through the porous formation and concentrated in the lower sections, giving them a redder tint. Ranger Al Warneke explained to me that the oxides also helped cement the quartz grains into a harder rock. The upper, white sections of the Navajo are much softer. "You can take some of the white rock in your hand," he said, "and crumble it between your fingers."

Climbers focus most of their big-wall efforts on the harder, red sections of the Navajo. "Large slabs of the white rock will break away when you don't expect it," said rock climber Alex Harris. "It will skateboard out from underneath your feet." Sandstone climbing, he said, has created a tight-knit community at Zion, without the arrogance he has sometimes found among those who climb on good rock. "We look out for each other," he told me. "The Navajo sandstone teaches you humility."

Moving up a ridge below Deertrap Mountain, we pass scattered ponderosa pines, their exposed roots twisting into the rock. Winds funnel through the notch between the rim pinnacles, stripping branches on the windward sides, leaving half-trees. "Stunted ponderosa is characteristic of Zion's slickrock," Bob says.

The pitch steepens, but the Navajo sandstone gives us enough friction to keep scrambling up. Reaching a knife-edge ridge, we cross to the base of the top cliffs. Somewhere nearby lies a zigzag route Bob once found while climbing down from the summit. We traverse along a ledge looking for it, and begin to work our way up at the most likely spot. Since we're in the white Navajo, the greatest hazard is the crumbly sandstone. Each foothold and handhold has to be tested.

"It goes, but there's a rather airy step," Tony calls back as he scouts ahead for the best route. A sheer cliff drops to a long slope falling hundreds of feet to Pine Creek below. We pass packs to each other to keep from being thrown off balance when we make the lateral move—not difficult but exposed. Once committed, each of us climbs carefully and without hesitation, stretching across a break in the ledge.

Completing the short traverse, we begin negotiating a series of vertical cracks up a broken rock face. Clumps of mountain mahogany and squawbush block the route in places, forcing us to auger our way through the brush. In other spots, sand has collected above plugs of twigs and pine needles caught in the fissures. These sandholds erode as quickly as we climb.

More sky than rock begins to open overhead as we near the top. "Got it!" I hear Tony shout from above, screened by the caprock. "I've topped out."

Bob and I join Tony on the summit. To the west, Zion Canyon drops into a wilderness of hanging stone. Massive half-domes and temples rim the great canyon. The East Temple stands before us on our side of the gorge; the West Temple dominates the far side. Immense mural walls, stained with streaks of red and black, fall a sheer 1,500 feet below the dentate peaks. At Zion, rock is transformed into flowing lines of pure geometry in a rare combination of power and grace.

Immediately before us, a chasm separates Deertrap from the back wall of a peak called Twin Brothers. Layers of sandstone feather into each other in clearly exposed crossbedding, the strata undulating in smooth curves. I had forgotten how strangely beautiful this country can be. Each time I return, I wonder why I have been away so long.

Ravines to the south trench the white-domed uplands; *(Continued on page 60)*

Water—at times tranquil, at times tumultuous—continues to shape Zion Canyon. The chief architect of this world of vertical walls and plunging abysses is the Virgin River (opposite), here cleaving a 1,500-foot-high sandstone defile called The Narrows. Each year the river, swollen by springtime freshets and summertime torrents, may carry more than a million tons of rock and sediment on its way south to join the Colorado at Lake Mead. North Creek (below), a Virgin River tributary, erodes a fracture in the larger channel carved in the sandstone of the Kayenta formation.

FOLLOWING PAGES: Water seeping through Zion's porous rock formations nourishes a perennial garden of maidenhair ferns.

high ridges and beehive rocks hide the deep narrows of Parunaweap Canyon, cut by the East Fork of the Virgin River. After exploring the Paunsaugunt Plateau in 1872, Powell descended into the Parunaweap Narrows. "Everywhere this deep passage is dark and gloomy," he wrote, "and resounds with the noise of rapid waters."

Following the flat summit of Deertrap northward, we trail through stands of ponderosa and juniper, tracking red-mud prints across mounds of old snow. The color comes from the Temple Cap formation—the same capstone on the far side of the canyon that stains the Altar of Sacrifice bloodred.

The last storm had passed a week ago, enough time for the snow to settle and for a good crust to form on the surface. Deer tracks, shaped like narrow valentine-heart cutouts, trail across the snow. In places they mark where deer have floundered, breaking through to their bellies with each leap. In earlier times, Paiute trapped mule deer here by driving them across a narrow neck connecting Deertrap with the main plateau. Then, blocking the escape route, the hunters moved in for the kill.

"Way back, my tribe always followed the deer herds," said Paiute elder Clifford Jake. Two days before, I had driven with him into the Kolob Canyons in northern Zion. "They went up the mountains in the spring, down in the fall. No more. The Great Spirit put the first people here on Mother Earth—gave us our food, gave us our water, gave us our life. Now it all has been taken away from us."

Nomadic bands of Southern Paiute ranged from California to Colorado when the first Spanish explorers crossed the Colorado Plateau in the mid-1600s. Anasazi farmers had abandoned the area hundreds of years before, leaving a few scattered ruins in the Zion country and a few enigmatic symbols pecked into the cliff faces. In the mid-1800s, Mormon settlers found an estimated 1,000 Paiute living in scattered groups along the Virgin River from the mouth of Zion Canyon to the Colorado River. Within a century they had disappeared, wiped out by starvation and disease. The last member of the Virgin River band died in 1945.

Clifford Jake, often called upon as a traditional spokesman for the tribe, is one of the last survivors of the Indian Peak band that now lives in Cedar City. His cowboy hat shaded a broad face with a low-curving mouth set off by eyes that twinkled when he spoke.

"Way back, people used to live here," he said. To reach the Kolob Canyons, hidden behind the Hurricane Cliffs, we followed a road through the gap cut by Taylor Creek. "They called this Brother-in-Law Stream. They lived here, even if there was no green, even if it was pretty rough. They pulled rocks together, stuck brush up to keep the wind out." The nomadic Paiute lived in temporary brush shelters sometimes covered with bark or animal skins.

As the road rounded a bend, a massive headland of red sandstone rose before us. The map named the promontory Tucupit Point—an English rendering of a Paiute word. Clifford tried the word on his tongue, giving it several pronunciations before finding the way to say it. "Mountain lion," he said, "it means mountain lion."

Kolob itself is an unusual name, but it's not Paiute and not Native American. Wes Larsen, a retired professor living in the nearby town of Toquerville, once explained it to me. According to Mormon doctrine, Kolob refers to the star nearest God's home—a place where a day is equal to a thousand years on earth.

The Mormons knew the Kolob from an early date, Wes said. He is a descendant of Parley P. Pratt, an apostle of the Mormon Church who led an exploring party into the region in 1849. The first Mormon to build a cabin in the Kolob was John D. Lee, said Wes. An adopted son of Mormon leader Brigham Young, Lee led settlers into the canyon country and established the settlement of Fort Harmony at the base of the Hurricane Cliffs. By the late 1850s he was on the run from federal authorities.

Facing an invasion by the United States Army in 1857, the Mormon militia and their Indian allies ambushed a wagon train near Cedar City, at a place called Mountain Meadows. Seeking revenge for earlier persecution, they executed 120 California-bound emigrants, sparing only the youngest children. Implicated as a leader of the massacre two years later, Lee rode into the Kolob country to hide out.

"He found a place on La Verkin Creek," Wes said, "and built a cabin. He could be on the ridge above Fort Harmony in an hour's ride. From up there he could look directly down on the settlement, where one of his wives would light a signal fire. Two campfires meant trouble; one meant it was safe."

Other leaders of the massacre hid with Lee, Wes believes, and used a trail through the Kolob linking Fort Harmony to the town of Virgin near Zion Canyon. The Mormons kept knowledge of the trail to themselves, using it as an escape route when federal marshals began enforcing the anti-polygamy laws. "I'm sure all the polygamists used the trail," he said.

Twenty years after Mountain Meadows, a firing squad executed Lee for his role in the massacre. In 1990 hundreds of his descendants and those of the Mountain Meadows victims gathered for a memorial service to heal old wounds. At a ceremony in Cedar City, Clifford Jake offered a Paiute prayer for both sides of the conflict.

As we continued up the Kolob road, Clifford said the Paiute who traveled into the canyons sometimes heard a frightening noise at night, an almost human screaming. "It's Kinasava—the one who herds the deer," he said. "It is like a small human with lots of fur. They move real fast, you only get a look before they disappear. They got a healing power." I asked him if he had seen one. "No," he said, "but I'd sure like to."

The road topped Lee Pass overlooking Timber Creek and the deeply etched face of the Kolob Plateau. We pulled into a turnoff opposite the narrow, still snow-choked canyons that fingered into the massive cliffs of red sandstone.

"The old Indian people, they mostly lived down below," Clifford said, "but they came up here to camp and get medicines, to hunt. In this place they had a *feeling*." He drew out the last word, charging it with meaning. "They lived somewhere not because it was easy to find food but because they were free. There's a spiritual feeling to it. When they came here, they had a *feeling*."

At the other end of the park on the edge of Zion Canyon, Bob, Tony, and I reach the north end of Deertrap Mountain. We look down to the North Fork of the Virgin, 2,400 feet below. The river loops smoothly around Angels Landing, its waters a dead green that blends with the winter grass and the bare limbs of the cotton-woods. Just to our north, a cluster of hoodoos tops the summit of the Great White Throne. High above it stretch the Pink Cliffs on the rim of the Markagunt Plateau.

Rockfalls have left scars on the cliff faces across the canyon. Slides happen with some frequency. After a heavy rain in 1981, 15,000 tons of rock split off from a cliff across from the Narrows Trail. Falling 1,000 feet, the rocks created hurricane-force winds and hit with such impact that debris shot across the canyon floor and climbed 20 feet up the far wall.

Backtracking a short distance, we pick up a trail that leads across the neck to the main plateau. But once in the open, it disappears beneath deep snow. As the day warms, we begin breaking through the crust. I take less than a dozen steps before sinking knee-deep in the wet snow. Taking a few more, I post-hole again, and then again. We have three and a half miles to go before dropping into the warmer reaches of Echo Canyon. I slog across the plateau in waterlogged boots, my feet beginning to numb.

We stop for a rest later in a thicket of Gambel oak surrounded by open flats. As we sit, I become aware of the quiet. All the rumbles, hums, and buzzes that our way of life has brought into existence have been left behind. The ear waits, expecting to hear what is no longer there.

With a couple of hours of walking still ahead of us, we're soon back at it, trudging along an old wagon road. By now everyone has wet boots. We take a trail that branches toward the rim of Echo Canyon. Bob spots a fresh set of mountain lion tracks heading toward the plateau where the deep drifts will slow a fleeing deer.

Snowbanks remain where the trail angles into the shadow of a north-facing wall. With sheer cliffs below, we pick our way along the icy ledge until the trail turns a corner. Suddenly everything is clear and dry—not a patch of snow anywhere.

Switchbacking down a steep ridge, we reach the canyon floor. There's a feeling of release as we leave the plateau and pass from winter into spring. The air is noticeably warmer, birds sing from a tall ponderosa nearby, and a lone fly buzzes overhead. We stop for a moment in the warm sunlight by a flowing creek that will dry up later in the season.

Leaning back on my elbows, I rest on a sandy bank covered with pine needles and enclosed on all sides by vertical rock. Clifford Jake was right about this

country—there is a feeling to it. The hard-edged beauty is part of it. And part of it is what the rock itself teaches—a geologist's sense of time, a rock climber's respect.

Cairns lead us down the canyon to meet the paved East Rim Trail. I've forgotten that many of Zion's main trails have been paved. To my eye it looks overbuilt, but Tony says the pavement is needed. The concrete prevents the pounding of feet from reducing the soft sandstone to loose sand. As the trail enters a slot in the cliffs, it skirts soaring walls speckled with lucid green moss. Out of sight below, the stream curls and drops, echoing deep-throated through a chamber of fluted walls.

Passing through the narrows, we break into the open on the cliff above Weeping Rock. Water percolates down through the porous Navajo sandstone until it reaches a resistant layer of shale below. Prevented from sinking deeper, the water moves horizontally and seeps from the open face of the cliff in a steady shower. In the warmer months, Weeping Rock supports a hanging garden of plants such as maidenhair fern, monkey flower, and columbine.

A few more turns of the trail and we pass the first patch of spring grass. Descending the last cliff, we leave the daylight behind and enter the evening shadows that have begun to rise from the depths of Zion Canyon.

On the last stretch of trail, I ask Tony about The Maze in Canyonlands National Park. He has explored that country in all seasons and advises me to see it soon to avoid the heat. He says to let him know when I want to go, and he'll join me.

We reach the canyon floor where the trail ends in a nearly empty parking lot. A man in his late sixties stands next to his camper, talking to a young ranger. "The last time I was here," he says, "was 30 years ago."

"It's changed quite a bit, hasn't it?" asks the ranger.

"*I've* changed quite a bit," he says, "but I don't know about *it.*"

Weeping walls feed Zion's springs and streams—as at Spirit Seep (opposite) and in the grotto-like Double Arch Alcove on Taylor Creek's Middle Fork. Percolating through porous sandstone, groundwater from the plateaus high above emerges as springs and seeps because it encounters a deeply buried layer of impermeable shale.

FOLLOWING PAGES: Thrusting 2,600 feet above the Virgin River, the Watchman's sandstone ramparts guard the southern approach to Zion park.

THE WORLD OF
CANYON COUNTRY
WILDLIFE

The mountain lion, also called puma or cougar, prefers the rugged high country regions of the Colorado Plateau, where mule deer are its staple prey. Shy and elusive, many cats have been given radio collars so scientists can monitor them in the wild.

N avajo tradition names thirteen worlds of existence, each on a different level. When the Navajo emerged from level four, the Dark Underworld, into level five, the Red Underworld, everything they saw was glossy red, and there were no birds, plants, or trees.

People who have never visited the Colorado Plateau may think of it in the same way that the Navajo saw the Red Underworld—a barren place of desert and red rock and not much else. But a close look will reveal a mosaic of life zones, or ecological communities. Each community covers a particular geographic area and is determined by climate—a combination of precipitation and temperature. Climate influences where plants will grow and where animals will live. In canyon country, which ranges from the highest plateaus, at over 10,000 feet—high enough to catch rain and snow and support pine and fir forests—to canyon bottoms at under 2,500 feet, differences in elevation create a wide diversity of life zones.

Over millions of years, water created the landscape of the plateau region, carving through flat rock to create deep canyons. But much of that water does not stay, and most of the water-carved canyons are now dry. Rain and snow-melt run quickly over the hard surfaces and are carried away in streams and rivers or collect in precious potholes. Survival on the Colorado Plateau comes only with water. Plants grow where water collects. Animals come to eat the plants and each other and to drink the water.

There doesn't have to be a lot of water. Less than ten inches a year is all it takes to sustain life in the desert, the lowest in elevation of the Colorado Plateau's three chief ecological communities. The lowest regions of the Colorado Plateau, at the bottom of the canyons, are the driest. Here lie low desert, slick-rock, and badlands. The only perennial plants that grow are cactuses and desert shrubs such as rabbitbrush, blackbrush, and snakeweed. Collared lizards, feeding on insects, live among the rocks. Canyon mice, which eat mostly seeds, can

A summer storm (left) brings lightning and rain to Monument Valley. The sandy soil supports desert brush and grasses, lizards, ravens, and coyotes. Ice coats a ponderosa pine (right) at El Morro National Monument, New Mexico. Winter ice and snow from above will melt to feed a large pool nearby, hollowed from rock by centuries of rain and snow. The rest will be absorbed by the soil or get carried away as runoff. Ponderosas favor an elevation of 8,000 feet or higher, where they can find sufficient moisture. The most common pine in North America, ponderosas can grow to a height of 130 feet, sometimes reaching out of deep rock chasms toward the sunlight.

climb even the steepest slickrock and sometimes colonize mesa tops. At dusk, desert cottontails hop about, looking for grass and plants, while at night, snakes hunt for mice, hawks hunt for snakes, and coyotes—which also range much higher—look for just about anything that moves.

In the middle zone, slightly more precipitation falls, and there is more soil to hold more of it. Piñon and juniper cling to the sides of cliffs, their roots breaking through cracks in the rocks, where moisture concentrates. They grow densely in places, creating a gray-green dwarf forest that can cover miles. Piñon jays and piñon mice forage for pine nuts; gray foxes and bobcats prey on rodents and ground-nesting birds.

Higher up, in the high plateaus that resemble flat-topped mountains, there is more rain and abundant snow. The bark of the aspen is a favorite food of rabbits, while shrubs and grasses provide browse for deer and bighorn sheep. Alpine meadows are home to yellow-bellied marmots. Nuthatches, chickadees, and juncos live in the pine forests.

Streams and rivers, cutting through rock, run into the desert to create mini-oases on both banks. Along the streams, Fremont cottonwood, box elder, tamarisk, and willow grow. Springs trickle out along contacts between hard and soft rock formations. On cliffsides, rock seeps support luxurious hanging gardens of maidenhair ferns, orchids, yellow and scarlet monkey flowers, and columbines. Canyon tree frogs and toads frequent pools, and dragonflies hover over streams that contain snail species found nowhere else in the world. Beavers gnaw on the bark of cottonwoods and willows. Where there is a pool or stream, animals such as the wood rat stop to drink, and predators—rattlesnakes, hawks, striped skunks—appear to hunt the wood rats. Whenever there is rain and snow, water collects in rock depressions called potholes. Mosquitoes, shrimp, and water beetles hatch and grow, providing food for hungry toads, spiders, and dragonflies.

Prickly pear (above) grows at lower elevations, easily surviving winter cold. In Monument Valley (right), horsetails stand in a storm-flooded sand bed. An agave (opposite, bottom right) flowers only once in many years. Juniper trees (bottom center) survive by growing in rock cracks to take advantage of runoff. Their berry-like cones provide food for birds, mice, and bears. Another agave species (below) grows slowly for 10 to 50 years or so, until one spring it sends up a huge stalk tipped with nectar-filled flowers, then dies.

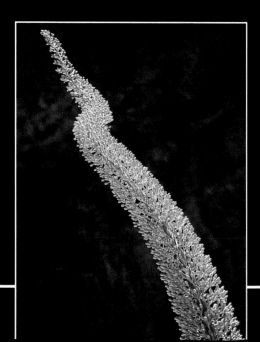

*A desert bighorn sheep (above) roams
the canyons and plateaus searching for
browse. Desert bighorn that aren't near
a lake or stream have been known to
kick open cactus to get water. A
fledgling spotted owl (opposite, top)
rests at the mouth of a cave. At night, its
parents will search the wooded canyons
for mice and other prey. A young coyote
(opposite, middle) rests at the mouth of
its den, possibly an abandoned fox or
badger hole. A desert spiny lizard
(opposite, bottom) keeps cool and
hides from predators on a canyon rock
ledge. Hiding in a tree cavity, a desert
cottontail (left) grooms an ear.*

A pothole (opposite) will disappear within days or weeks of the rainfall or snowmelt that created it. In that short time, the tadpole shrimp (left) hatches, matures, lays eggs, and dies. A Great Basin rattlesnake (below) visits the pothole for water and a possible meal. House finches (above) find cool shelter and a drink at a water seep.

Hedgehog, or claret cup, cactus (opposite, bottom) is an important source of food for honey ants. The ants remove the forest of stamens from the cactus flower (opposite, top) to lap up the nectar in the "well." Then they carry the nectar back to the nest and regurgitate it to other workers called honeypots. The sluggish honeypots (above) hang from the ceiling of the nest and store the nectar in their abdomens, which can expand to the size of small grapes. The honeypots regurgitate the nectar when hungry members of the colony signal them, perhaps in a time of drought.

Young aspen trees (above) on the North Rim of the Grand Canyon endure in spite of rough pruning by hungry deer. Aspens thrive at high elevations with plentiful rain. They are pioneer trees, growing in logged or burned-over areas or at the edge of forests. An elderly hackberry tree (opposite, top) survives the long intervals between rains by growing in a sandy wash, the dry bed of a stream that floods intermittently. A mule deer (opposite, bottom) browses in a high meadow. The deer gets its name from the large, mulelike ears, which help detect danger at long range. Its favorite foods are twigs, leaves, grasses, and mushrooms. Mule deer may climb hard snowbanks to nibble on aspen catkins high above the ground.

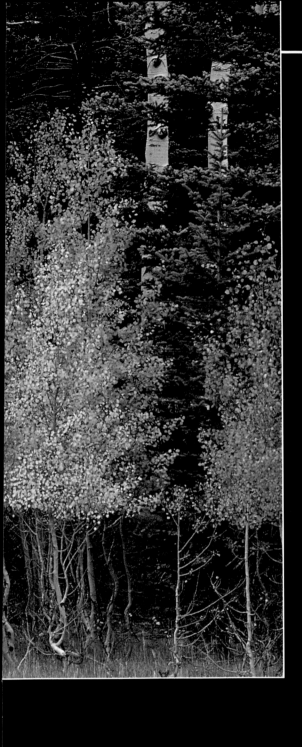

A migrating rufous hummingbird
drinks nectar from a wild columbine,
common in rock seeps in the canyons.
The rufous will visit many of these
plants in a day, attracted by the bright
red and yellow flowers. It also eats
spiders and insects.

CANYON
HEARTLANDS

Ribs of Sandstone, Spires of Shale, Crystal Mountains, Windows in the Rock

Washes run muddy red as we make our way to the Land of Standing Rocks. Clouds smolder above the Orange Cliffs where dark streaks of runoff glisten on the slickrock faces. Spring rains have recharged the canyon lands, drawing out the deeper colors. "It's a dynamic time to be in the desert," says back-road guide Jani Roper.

After six hours of jeep-trail driving, Jani stops to check another rough turn in the road—much the way a river runner scouts a rapid. She wears a pair of green mud boots in case the truck bogs down somewhere along the way.

My friends Tony Williams and Terry Gustafson decide this is a good place to stretch their legs. We'll be doing a lot more walking in the days to come. Our plan is to traverse Canyonlands National Park from The Maze to The Needles, crossing the Colorado River with light rafts. Later I'll cross the Waterpocket Fold on a second probe into the heart of the canyon country, linking Capitol Reef National Park with Glen Canyon National Recreation Area.

Putting the truck in low gear, Jani descends the rocky ledge. If she cuts the wheels a few inches too far to the right, the truck will slip over the edge of a ravine. Throwing it into reverse in the middle of the curve and forward again, she clears the drop and picks up the walkers.

A few more bouncing miles and we find ourselves among the Standing Rocks. Scattered spires of Organ Rock shale tower above the benchlands, their

PRECEDING PAGES: North Window frames Turret Arch in The Windows section of Arches National Park, Utah. Rock, weathered into arches, pinnacles, buttes, hoodoos, and a multitude of other forms, lies at the heart of the canyon country.

Afternoon light catches a runner on the spine of a rock fin in Arches. Weathering and erosion shape parallel fractures into massive blades of Entrada sandstone. Further thinning can perforate an upright slab, forming a natural arch or window.

solitary forms silhouetted against the sky. The road takes us past a freestanding wall, 200 feet high and twice as long. Enclosing nothing, surrounded by empty space, it gives scale to the immensities of sky and rock. Beyond it lies The Maze. We stop and walk to the edge. Cliffs of one gorge stack behind another as far as we can see. Each canyon branches again and again like the tangled limbs of a dead juniper.

That night we camp beneath an overhanging ledge in case the rains return. Smoke from old campfires has blackened the ceiling, and red flakes of jasper spill down the sandy slope in front. Darkness comes slowly. Each week the sky holds the light noticeably longer than the last as the seasons shift.

The Maze lies below the level of the surrounding tablelands, unseen from camp. Our talk keeps circling back to it. Tony has made a number of trips into its canyons before. He spends much of his time exploring the Colorado Plateau, choosing to live in a small town close to both the Grand Canyon and Zion. Terry, who has worked for years as a backcountry ranger in the Sierra Nevada, also has wandered through parts of the rock labyrinth. For me it's an unknown.

After breaking camp the next morning, Jani leaves us on the edge of The Maze and returns to town. Terry, Tony, and I contour along the white rimrock looking for a way below. Most of our gear remains behind at base camp. Tony wears a white canvas hat that can be stuffed into a day pack; Terry a wide-brim straw hat for maximum shade. "Onward and downward," says Terry as we begin the descent.

Cairns mark a serpentine route, threading from ledge to ledge down layers of Cedar Mesa sandstone. One side canyon feeds into another, and then another as we descend. Since we plan to return to camp by a different route, I pay little attention to the intersecting canyons, a lapse I'll regret later.

We enter a large tributary of Horse Canyon that the map leaves unnamed, but that hikers call Pictograph Fork. Turning downstream once again, we make no

effort to count the bends as the canyon descends in tight meanders. The sandy floor lies untracked, washed clean by recent rains.

Where the gorge widens, a haze of green covers the branches of a stunted cottonwood tree just beginning to leaf. Tufts of Indian ricegrass grow beneath it on stems so fine the seeds appear to float. Just beyond, the canyon wall curves into the full sunlight. I can make out a faint row of ghostly figures painted on the wall in dark reds. Moving to the foot of the cliff, we stare up at strange, elongated beings—armless, faceless, and as unmoving as standing rocks.

At the far end of the panel, known as the Harvest Scene, the pictographs become more animated. One commanding figure, perhaps a shaman, reaches out an open hand. A growth of ricegrass shoots from a fingertip. A rabbit runs down an arm, and a bird glides by. Bent under baskets, two humans gather seed grass.

Archaeologists believe Archaic gatherers and hunters painted these visionary scenes, but have no reliable dates. Estimates range from more than 5,000 years old to less than 2,000. Whatever the date, the Harvest Scene evokes the hidden world of these early maze dwellers, where the natural and supernatural merged.

"Doodling or deep meaning, what do you think?" Tony asks.

"I'm of the deep meaning school," says Terry.

Leaving the painted cliff, we enter a wider canyon leading to The Maze Overlook Trail. We find the trail heading up a ridge with handholds cut into cliffs at key points. Scrambling up a steep face, we keep as much boot sole in contact with the rough sandstone as possible. "The coefficient of friction," Terry says, "that's all that's keeping us up."

The three of us continue past hammerheaded columns of rock to The Maze Overlook. Below us, deep gorges slice vertically through alternating bands of red and white. The eye reads horizontal, but the pit of the stomach says vertical.

Storms often sweep Arches' plateau country in winter. At the Devils Garden, a snowy Utah juniper (opposite) stands before an arch spanning an ephemeral pool. Icicles (right) frame a freestanding wall known as the Organ.

FOLLOWING PAGES: Venus and a waning crescent moon rise above Balanced Rock, silhouetted against the dawn sky in Arches. A weathered pedestal of softer stone supports an immense boulder weighing more than 3,500 tons. Author Edward Abbey recorded his life as a park ranger living nearby in the classic Desert Solitaire.

A touch of vertigo happens when the two messages mix. "This is just such incredibly confusing country," Tony says, scanning the jigsaw canyons below.

Turning back, Tony and I take a climbing route directly off the point. Terry chooses the trail, longer but surer. All goes well as Tony and I work from bench to bench, until we reach a slickrock face dropping into a cleft of empty space. Slightly inclined and without handholds, the wall has a thin bed of harder rock protruding just enough to hold a foot. Relying mostly on friction, Tony eases across to a wide ledge and waits for me to follow. I sidestep along the micro-ledge, fighting the natural tendency to hug the rock. The secret is to stay upright so that the line of gravity pushes your feet against the rock and not away from it. "Vertical, stay vertical," Tony coaches as I pass the critical point.

We soon reach the floor of the main canyon and join Terry. High above, two hikers make their way across the ridge—the first people we've seen. They walk bent under their backpacks like ancient harvest figures stooped beneath burden baskets.

By now it's late afternoon, and we're faced with a decision. We have enough time to attempt a high route, or we can play it safe and return to camp the way we came. The consensus is to try the new route. Something about the intricate topography draws us deeper into the sandstone maze.

A path leads us into an alcove and ends at the base of a bald slope. We scramble up it and climb from one shelf to the next. But an overhanging cliff near the top of the gorge keeps us from reaching the tablelands above. Tony gives it a try, finally pulling himself over the bulging lip. The way above looks clear, he reports.

Terry checks the climb and decides it's too risky. Studying it from above, Tony doesn't think he can climb down safely. The cliff divides us. Since it's too late in the day to split the party and let Tony go on alone, Terry and I lug a juniper log partway up the cliff. We set one end of it in a small niche and lean the other against the upper cliff. Tony secures the free end with parachute cord.

Working my way up, I use the rock face as much as possible. Terry starts to climb once I'm on top. Just as he reaches the upper edge of the cliff, the log breaks free, sending him crashing onto the slope below.

For a long moment he lies unmoving before I hear him say he's okay. He sits up slowly, making sure nothing is broken. With some difficulty, Tony and I climb down and check his injuries. He's badly scraped and bruised but able to continue. We turn back and descend the way we came, finding the route down harder to negotiate than the climb up. Our chances of reaching the rim by dark are now slim.

Back on the floor of the canyon, we enter Pictograph Fork and begin retracing our morning route. The canyon, deep in shadows, looks changed. The walls stand higher, the gorge narrower. We pass places we don't remember seeing before. Another party has passed through, covering our tracks.

Terrain looks different when approaching it from another direction, but here the geographic complexity heightens the effect. Reaching a likely prong of the canyon, we stop and debate whether or not to take it. Unsure, we press on. If we're wrong, night will catch us below the rim, forcing us to bivouac until morning.

Reaching a window of The Doll House, an intrepid climber stands among soaring rock walls and spires clustered on the rim of Cataract Canyon. The Doll House lies in the remote Maze country of Canyonlands National Park, Utah.

The canyon seems much longer than it did on the way in. I begin to think we must have missed the turn in the flat twilight. But as we round a bend, a herd of mule deer startles and runs up a side canyon. Suddenly all the pieces fall into place—cut bank, curve of canyon. It's the fork we came down that morning. We turn up it without pausing, needing to cover as much ground as possible before full dark.

A doe and a yearling watch us from a shelf above. Ears stiff, they stand dead still until the young deer twitches, breaking the spell. Both spring into action. The yearling hesitates a moment at the lip of the cliff just as the mother leaps past. Together, they bound down the broken slope as smoothly as flowing water.

We find the last fork in the final moments of daylight. Zigzagging up to the rim, the three of us top out beneath a wide night sky. We've left The Maze behind but still have a long road to walk before reaching camp. Tired, we keep to the jeep trail to avoid getting lost in the moonless night. Our pace matches the slow procession of stars shifting overhead.

"You know," Terry says, as we walk down the dark road, "there's nowhere I'd rather be but here."

"How about camp?" I ask, surprised.

"We'll get there at just the right time," he says.

Leaving camp the next morning under full packs, we head into a new section of The Maze. Each of us carries a deflated raft lashed onto the top of packs already bulging with camping gear, food, and water. "It feels like an albatross around my neck," Terry says.

Tony scouts ahead and locates a route down Shot Canyon where remnants of an old horse trail traverse a smooth drop. Trail builders roughened the slope enough to hold smaller stones, then covered them with large slabs placed so carefully they hold to the cliff by friction alone. The stone steps appear to float down the rock face, as if the weight of a single footstep will tip the balance and send them tumbling below. We descend cautiously.

Once on the canyon floor, the pathway cuts across a patch of cryptobiotic soil. Scarlet flowers of an Indian paintbrush open against the black organic crust. We take care to stay on the trail. Park biologist Jayne Belnap told me it takes decades for disturbed cryptobiotic soil to fully recover. The sticky fibers of cyanobacteria, what used to be called blue-green algae, weave through the sand. Together with lichens, algae, and fungi, they form an erosion-resistant crust. Jayne stressed the importance of cryptobiotic soils for Utah's cold deserts. "Over the years," she said, "they are what holds the whole system together."

Shadows thin as the day grows warmer. We ascend a red-banded cliff, passing up our packs to a higher ledge. Crossing into Water Canyon, we find springwater curling from a stand of cottonwoods and trickling over a 40-foot drop. We stop to rest by the stream. Leaving the creek, we head up the far wall and enter a grassy pocket encircled by weathered pinnacles. Dumping our packs, we walk to the rim above the confluence. The Green River makes a tight bend 1,700 feet beneath us. Its turbid waters loop between the cliffs of the inner canyon as if (Continued on page 104)

Snowcapped La Sal Mountains tower above tiny vehicles and the massive slickrock domes of Behind the Rocks country near Canyonlands National Park.

Visitors to Canyonlands have discovered a variety of ways to experience the park's backcountry. Mountain bikers descend the rugged Shafer Trail Road that twists down the face of Island in the Sky as a storm cloud moves across the gorge of the Colorado River. Far below, near the water's edge, opera singers give a wilderness performance in an improbable setting. A jet boat transported the piano down the Colorado River to a landing where it was hoisted up the riverbank with a block and tackle.

FOLLOWING PAGES: Mesa Arch hangs on the brink of cliff-cut Island in the Sky. The angular mesa rises above a slickrock wilderness of monoliths, weathered benchlands, and the confluence of the Green and Colorado Rivers, deep in the canyons below.

Pinnacles and pillared walls weather from the White Rim (left) in Canyonlands' Monument Basin. White Rim sandstone rises a thousand feet above the Green and Colorado Rivers in the Island in the Sky country. A broad bench towers 1,200 feet above White Rim. To the southeast, petroglyphs (below) crowd a cliff at Newspaper Rock Historical Monument. Over some 3,000 years, Indians—and settlers—pecked a profusion of figures into the dark desert varnish, leaving a record whose meaning largely remains elusive. The figures of horses must have been made after the Spanish introduced them into North America in the late 16th century.

PRECEDING PAGES: Rancher Heidi Redd takes a rare break from daily chores that begin before dawn. She raises cattle on the Dugout Ranch near Canyonlands and works to protect the fragile land from development.

lost in a labyrinth. The Green merges with the Colorado and disappears just beyond, swallowed by the inner gorge. John Wesley Powell climbed up from the river at this point. He looked across the canyonscape, so different from what he had left behind in Illinois. "Wherever we look," he wrote, "there is but a wilderness of rocks."

Returning to our packs, we make camp at the base of a mounded cliff that rises overhead like a storm cloud turned to stone. The gorge of the Colorado River falls away before us with The Needles forming a ragged skyline to the east. To the north, Island in the Sky mesa lifts above the confluence.

Night falls clear and windless. I lie back beneath a river of stars bending to the horizon. Dark limbs of an old juniper finger upward on one side; on the other, sand fills a hollow in the lunar slickrock. Without warning, a streak of light slices across the night sky, tracing a brief arc. A meteor.

Millions of years ago a meteorite may have hit what is now the Island in the Sky, forming a deep crater at Upheaval Dome. Concentric rings of rock surround the impact site, where strata flare upward in red and buff cliffs, squeezed into puckers and eroded into jagged fins. Fractured beds tilt skyward at the center of the depression, 500 feet below.

Geologists do not agree on how Upheaval Dome formed, but Gene Shoemaker has no doubts. "It's one of the most beautifully exposed impact structures in the world," the astrogeologist said to me on an earlier visit.

Shoemaker sat on the rim of Upheaval Canyon, in the dome's center, debating the structure's origin with other geologists. Wearing a khaki shirt and jeans with a silver Indian buckle, he presented a convincing argument for a meteorite impact. "There's a long history of things falling out of the sky and going bump in the night."

An asteroid 400 meters in diameter, Shoemaker estimated, crashed into the earth at that spot about 30 million years ago. It impacted with an explosive force equal to one-fifth of the world's nuclear arsenal. The rocks now exposed lay deeply buried at the time of the event; the actual impact crater eroded long ago.

Two other geologists countered Gene's explanation with reasoned arguments for less dramatic origins. Petroleum geologist Mike Hudec believed the crater formed when a buried salt dome separated from underlying salt beds over millions of years and subsequently eroded.

Rudi Kopf, now retired, held a subterranean column of slurry responsible for the unusual formation. Three geologists looked at one hole in the ground and saw three different forces at work.

Shoemaker passed around chunks of rock taken from deep within the crater. "It's shatter cone," he said. "You find it nowhere else but in an impact feature."

The next morning, Tony, Terry, and I make our way to a cluster of rock formations called The Doll House, passing a stone span called Beehive Arch. Cedar Mesa sandstone weathers into arches throughout Canyonlands, but the greatest concentration of natural arches in the world occurs beyond Island in the Sky in the Entrada sandstone of Arches National Park.

Earlier I had walked into the park's Devils Garden to see Landscape Arch,

PRECEDING PAGES: Power generated by nearby Glen Canyon Dam lights Lake Powell Marina at Wahweap, Arizona. Lake water, used for irrigation and hydropower, began covering 180 miles of canyon country upon completion of the dam in 1963.

perhaps for the last time. An opening 306 feet wide makes it possibly the world's longest rock span — Zion National Park also claims the title for Kolob Arch. Late in the summer of 1991, Landscape Arch began to pop and crack. A slab of Entrada sandstone, 60 feet long and four and a half feet thick, broke free and fell to the slope below. Rangers closed the trail beneath it, expecting the entire span to give way.

The trail to Landscape Arch took me between parallel fins of rock. From a low rise, I looked across to a far slope where a ribbon of sandstone, impossibly thin, floated between cliff walls. "Look!" said a visitor standing near me. "They're walking underneath. I guess the Park Service has stabilized it." But, because the danger of collapse had lessened with time, the rangers had reopened the trail. Even so, no one knows when the arch might fall.

Walking beneath the arch, I could see the fresh scar on the underside of the stone span. My pace picked up as I passed through its thin shadow. Standing on the far side, I looked at the open expanse framed by the slender arch. Nothing moved except for a lone raven, gliding effortlessly above the high desert.

Tony, Terry, and I enter The Doll House through a gap in a pinnacled wall that circles an open park. Clouds tower above us, as flat-bottomed and round-topped as the rock itself. A deep fissure splits a cliff near the trail. I explore the passageway, dark and cool. At a joint, a juniper grows surrounded by rock. Only indirect sunlight, glancing off the high stone walls, reaches it. The living tree survives in a world encompassed by stone.

The trail leaves The Doll House and drops abruptly to the Colorado River. It stitches down the face of the inner canyon to Spanish Bottom, a thousand feet below. Ranchers say it got its name from a branch of the Old Spanish Trail that crossed here. A spur of the Outlaw Trail later connected Butch Cassidy's hideout in Robbers Roost with the river crossing.

A few miles below the confluence, Spanish Bottom opens into a flat pocket bordered by the river on one side and pallid gray cliffs on the other. We hike across at midday, the sun unexpectedly hot for early April. Dead cottonwood trees stand above the tamarisk thicket on the bank, their trunks scorched by a fire that swept through a few years earlier. Compared with the smoothly curving sandstone above, the walls of the inner gorge look shattered, decayed. "It's a lonely place," says Terry.

Reaching the Colorado River, we inflate our rafts on a sandy bank. The dark waters push toward the head of Cataract Canyon just below. Tony has floated through here on a number of river trips. Around the corner, he tells us, lies a rapid that could capsize our boats in an instant.

Tony launches first in a raft the size of a bathtub and pulls hard for the far bank. He's across faster than we expected. Terry and I follow in our own boats. It's a long time since I've been on the Colorado with oars in my hands. It feels right. With my pack taking up half the space and the stubby oars flailing, I cross over.

As our boats dry on the rocks, we're faced with a decision. If we camp here, we'll have a sure source of water; if we continue, we'll have less ground to cover tomorrow but may not find water. With plenty of daylight left, we decide to push on and take our chances. Having filled all of our water containers and repacked the boats, we pass through the crumbled rock of Lower Red Lake Canyon. Pausing to rest at the top of the switchbacks, I glance back. The pinnacles across the river float remote and dreamlike on the cliffs above Spanish Bottom.

Lake Powell and the slickrock country bordering it draw 3.6 million visitors each year to boat, fish, hike, and water-ski within Glen Canyon National Recreation Area.

Once out of the inner canyon, we have no luck in finding water. The rimrock is too porous to form the good potholes found in Cedar Mesa sandstone. But the map indicates a spring in the next valley to the east. We decide to press on so we don't have to ration our water. We follow the trail across a narrow valley and reach the next, higher one at dusk. Tony sets down his pack and immediately goes to find the spring located a half mile away on the map. He returns in the dark, empty-handed. All he found was a dry hole choked with dry tumbleweed.

The water we pack isn't enough to completely rehydrate, to replenish what our bodies lost on the hike up from the river. We'll be cutting it close if we don't find more in the morning. Before turning in, we choose food that doesn't need to be cooked, eating lightly to cut back on water consumption.

Our dry camp is in The Grabens, a region of narrow, square-shouldered valleys formed when the underground movement of salt beds caused the surface rock to slump. A thick growth of tumbleweed covers the flat-bottomed valley. Heidi Redd, owner of the Dugout Ranch, ran cattle in The Grabens before it became part of the national park. She met me at ranch headquarters wearing a bib shirt and a tooled belt fastened with a silver buckle. A braid of blond hair fell from beneath a ten-gallon hat. She had been up since 4:00 in the morning, taking care of her cattle. "When you love your work," she said, "it doesn't matter."

The Dugout Ranch spreads along Indian Creek from Newspaper Rock to the park boundary at The Needles. A green ribbon of cottonwoods borders the creek, running between walls of Wingate sandstone. Stained red, the cliffs break into smooth, angular facets. Where the canyon widens, two pinnacled buttes called North Sixshooter and South Sixshooter aim their barrels skyward.

As we rode in her pickup to count calves, she talked about ranching. When she first arrived at the Dugout more than 25 years ago, she would round up cattle in The Needles and not see a single person. Canyonlands became a national park in 1964, and six years later the Park Service paved the road into The Needles.

"Did paving the road help preserve the park or invite overuse?" she asked. "We'd see only one car a week when it was still a rough dirt road. Now there's too many people. When you lose the feeling of being alone, you can't get in touch with the spirit of the land."

Heidi drove slowly through the cow pasture. She was pleased to find a new-born standing next to its mother, curious but ready to bolt. "They're so different from human babies," she said. "They're up on their legs and running from the start."

Returning to the ranch house she talked about her love for the land that has become her home. "I wish I was wise," she said, "but I'm just a cowgirl. It's like being a mother. I feel for the land, but at times I feel helpless. I have a deep feeling for the land I graze my cattle on and a great responsibility to nurture it."

She moves her cattle often, she said, before the grass is eaten down. "My heart aches for this country," she added, "it's so fragile. And it seems so much is being demanded of it. But there's never a morning when the sun starts coming up that I don't realize where I live and am thankful for it."

Tony, Terry, and I break camp as the predawn sky begins to gray above The Grabens. We want to cover as much ground as possible in the cool of the day to conserve our dwindling water. We'll wait and cook breakfast when we find more. The trail climbs to a pass overlooking Devils Lane. To the south stands The Needles, a sanctuary of clustered spires and pinnacle-rimmed grassy parks. As first light hits The Needles, we stop to rest.

We've entered the Cedar Mesa sandstone again, so our chances of finding a pothole are good. It's not so much the lack of water in the desert that worries people, but the uncertainty of water. The rains often come too early or too late, bringing too much moisture or not enough. In the dry weeks before they arrive, blue skies stretch flat and unchanging, day after day. And when the rain comes, it falls so hard it hurts the face. Dry washes flood; potholes overflow.

Approaching Devils Kitchen we find what we're looking for. A shaded pothole holds plenty of water. When you find a waterhole containing six or seven gallons and all you need is a few quarts, the abundance is overwhelming.

Each trip finds its own ending—sometimes before a destination is reached. We still have a few hours of walking ahead of us before getting to our car parked below Elephant Hill. But the hike draws to a close as we pass through the campground at Devils Kitchen followed by a pair of barking dogs and an anxious owner trying his best to call them off.

T wo weeks later, I'm walking alone on a remote trail in Capitol Reef National Park. The path disappears in a swampy seep, lost among matted cattail rushes and the ooze of black mud. A dense growth of willow blocks the way. Dropping to hands and knees, I crawl through the thicket and emerge deep in the rock-walled desert beyond.

Weaving through a patch of prickly pear, I glance back. The pocket of living green lies within the slickrock expanse of the Waterpocket Fold—an immense wave of upturned sandstone climbing 2,300 feet into the fading light. Dark storm clouds push across the crest as I head for a wall of knobby cliffs that might provide some shelter. I'm traveling light, without a tent or stove.

After spreading a sleeping bag beneath a dim petroglyph from some other century, I eat a handful of trail food. Dark clouds build above the cliff line across from camp. The Waterpocket Fold is unknown country for me, a place of uncertainty—it's exactly what I've come here to find.

Earlier in the day I had descended Halls Creek with three friends—Dave Slagle, Tom Suk, and Terry Gustafson. Our route took us along the foot of the Waterpocket Fold. This great flex in the earth's surface runs for a hundred miles along the length of Capitol Reef National Park. About midday we reached a point where the creek made a sharp bend to the west, away from the path of least resistance. It ran straight toward the steep flank of the Fold, drawn into the heart of the rock.

We entered Halls Creek Narrows, a passageway looping through the Navajo sandstone. At one bend the flowing water had hollowed out an alcove a hundred yards deep. We stopped there for lunch beneath a vault of rock that cut a parabolic curve across the blue sky. "This type of roof over my head is ideal," Terry said, sitting propped against his pack.

For three miles the canyon twisted in compound curves, alternating between broad amphitheaters and tight spots no wider than outstretched arms. We waded shallow gravel bars and passed packs across a chest-deep pool. A sweet aroma drifted through the canyon from plants flowering high above. At the end of the Narrows, I bid my companions good-bye and continued down the creek, passing the boundary between Capitol Reef and Glen Canyon National Recreation Area.

Now camped against a cliff wall in the gathering dark, I sit next to a scatter of flakes and potsherds left by Fremont Indians 800 years ago. Some 9,000 years before them, at the end of the Ice Age, nomadic bands of Paleo-Indians trekked across the Colorado Plateau, searching for mammoths. Larry Agenbroad, Northern Arizona University professor, believes they found them and hunted them to extinction.

When I entered his office before the trip, he cleared a stack of research papers from a chair so I could sit down. Jawbones and skulls of animals I didn't recognize covered the tops of file cabinets. Wearing jeans and cowboy boots, Larry talked about his team's ongoing study of Ice Age fauna in the national parks on the Colorado Plateau. Along the Colorado River near Canyonlands, the team has found mammoth remains not far from petroglyphs depicting mammoths. "I think that man and mammoth were contemporary in those canyons," he said.

In a cave in the Glen Canyon area, Agenbroad has excavated a site containing a thick layer of mammoth dung, 11,000 years old. These Ice Age elephants ate plants from a riparian forest now found only in the cooler and wetter reaches of the Henry Mountains, 4,000 feet higher. As the climate warmed, their environment shrank to a few islands high in the mountains. "We still have the same vegetation communities," he said, "but not the animals. I think there's no question that man did in the mammoths. It's just ridiculous to say that climate did it."

Mammoths had survived much harsher and milder *(Continued on page 114)*

During dry years with little runoff, the level of Lake Powell lowers, sometimes dramatically. In an inlet of Last Chance Bay, a lone houseboat moors under the smooth slopes of Navajo sandstone exposed by low water.

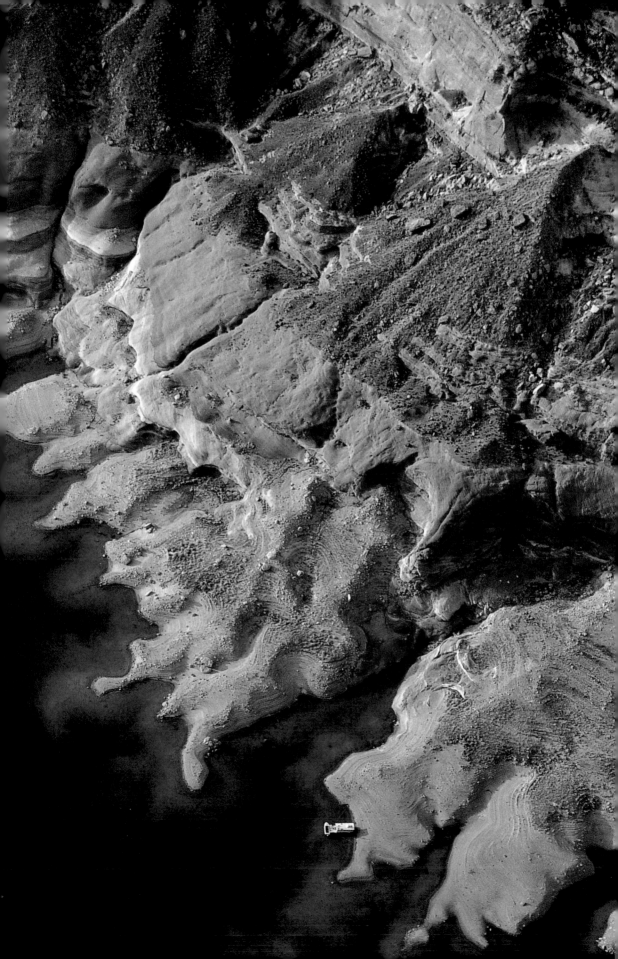

Clear waters of the Colorado River loop through the unflooded lower reaches of Glen Canyon as powerboats zip upstream. Released from Glen Canyon Dam seven miles above, the once muddy river now lures anglers to its trophy trout-fishing waters. Glen Canyon ends 15 miles below the dam at Lees Ferry, the historic river crossing and launch site for river trips entering the Grand Canyon. River flow, controlled by the dam, fluctuates in response to power demands from distant cities. Unexpected low water sometimes leaves downstream river runners high and dry.

PRECEDING PAGES: Kayakers paddle into a remote pocket of upper Lake Powell, exploring Dirty Devil Canyon, cut by the Dirty Devil River. Canoes and kayaks can probe narrow canyons along Lake Powell's almost 2,000 miles of shoreline.

climates in the past, he said. They were adapted to arctic and temperate climates—and they could migrate when conditions changed. "If they didn't like the weather," he said with a smile, "they would pack up their trunks and leave."

Agenbroad guards the locations of his sites to prevent vandalism—a necessary precaution, as I learned when I passed through the town of Escalante. A poster in the ranger station offered a reward for information leading to the arrest of those responsible for destroying a prehistoric site called Three Roof Ruin.

Park archaeologist Chris Kincaid told me the story. She said the wooden frame of a well-preserved Anasazi Indian ruin had stood beneath a protecting shelf of rock for eight centuries, undisturbed until boaters from Lake Powell dismantled the ancient beams and burned them in their campfire. "We're seeing destruction of all sites within a mile of the shoreline of Lake Powell," she said. "An incredible loss."

Breaking camp at first light, I cross Halls Creek and begin climbing the Waterpocket Fold. Slickrock ramps angle upward. They become cliffs on the reverse side. Facing upslope, a few of the cliffs trap runoff in deep water pockets. The route begins to steepen as it climbs bald spurs and drops into deep hollows. I walk a zigzag course, groping for the best route over the cross-bedded Navajo sandstone—"wavy and ripply," a cowboy once described it to me, "like it was all blowed in."

Working higher up a shoulder of slickrock, I stop a moment and look back. To the south, an arm of Lake Powell shines at the mouth of Halls Creek. To the north, clouds from last night's storm are passing the Henry Mountains, where snow seams the highest summit. During his first exploring trip, Powell named them the Unknown Mountains—they were the last unmapped mountains in the continental United States.

The Fold begins to level as I arrive on top, and the wind picks up. Canyons reaching up from the Escalante River finger into the narrow summit ridge. The river drains a pristine remnant of the Glen Canyon country, most of which lies beneath Lake Powell. The rimlands border a wild maze of rock, both rough and slick, that ranchers have given names like Death Hollow, Hells Backbone, and Scorpion Gulch.

Directly below, sheer cliffs of Wingate sandstone rim a branch of Stevens Canyon. During five days of exploring Stevens, Terry Gustafson found a single route connecting it with the top of the Fold. That's the one I have to find. Using a compass to set a course, I begin walking south on a line with Navajo Mountain, 35 miles away but appearing half that in the clear air.

Treading across sand ridges, I try to stay in washes or on bare rock to avoid the untracked crust. After a few miles, I spot the fork Terry marked on my map. But it's separated from me by tiers of cliffs. I make several probes trying to reach it, only to get rimrocked by sheer drops. I backtrack to the top of the Fold and try again. With water running low, I circle far to the east and approach it from a different angle. If this attempt fails, I'll have to return to Halls Creek, where I can find water.

I follow a sunken wash that might be the key to the puzzle. It leads between

Temple of the Sun climbs from the desert floor of Lower Cathedral Valley in the far northern corner of Utah's Capitol Reef National Park. Exposed layers of soft Entrada sandstone erode into jagged monoliths hundreds of feet high.

two cliffs, but ends abruptly. Turning back, I notice a fresh set of coyote tracks, the first tracks of any animal I've seen here. I follow them over a sand dune and down a break in the cliff. Below the barrier, the coyote veered from the logical course. Curious, I continue following its tracks for a short distance. They lead directly to a pothole of water—the ultimate reprieve in the desert. I tank up before pushing on.

The drainage soon intersects an old trail. I take it, descending the cliff wall to the canyon floor. Removing my pack, I lean back for a moment and settle into the contours of the rock. Flash floods have scoured the channel, leaving only bedrock and water and the sound of water trickling into deep green pools below.

Soon on my way again, I head down the canyon, drawn deeper into the rock. Detouring around a barrier fall, I follow a ledge halfway between the rim and the canyon floor. Smooth walls rise above, and a sheer cliff falls below. By the time I've walked a couple of miles, the angle of the light has shifted lower. Rocks begin to stand alone, distance takes on depth, colors turn fluid. Tiring, I decide to camp as soon as the long bypass brings me back to the creek bed.

But as the canyon makes another bend, the ledge I'm following suddenly ends. Fractured boulders and pulverized sandstone block the way ahead. A massive rockslide has buried the shelf under an unstable slope, balanced at the angle of repose. A red scar on the cliff face marks where a tremendous slab broke off and crashed into the canyon, covering the ledge and damming the gorge. A narrow lake fills the depths below, ending any chance of finding a lower route. I feel trapped. Even if I find a way through, I don't know what lies beyond.

The remaining light withdraws up the sides of the canyon. I decide to bivouac until morning, having reached a stage of tiredness when mistakes happen easily. I carry less than a quart of water. Backtracking a bit, I look for a level spot to camp. On the ledge below lies a runoff channel hollowed into basins. Unexpectedly, each holds water. I take a canteen and climb down to the largest hole.

Before filling the canteen, I pause a moment above the dark pool and stare at the reflection of sky and rimrock. The water stands as still as rock. The grain of rock enclosing the basin curves in whorls as fluid as water. On each side, the stone ledge flows in soft undulations. Caught by night on a remote slickrock bench, I'm content to be where I am.

S ome canyoneers claim The Maze is the heart of the canyon country. Others locate the heart at the confluence of the Green and Colorado Rivers or deep in the Grand Canyon. Ken Sleight, one of the first river guides on the Colorado Plateau, placed it elsewhere.

On my way to southern Utah, I stopped for an annual gathering of river runners near Lees Ferry, where Glen Canyon ends and Marble Canyon begins. That night Ken stood next to a bonfire telling stories about his 40 years of guiding.

"I was just a cowpoke before," he said, wearing a straw cowboy hat pulled snug across his forehead. Firelight reflected in his glasses as he talked. "The closest I'd come to a river was riding my horse through a swamp. I'm from the old school," he said with a smile, "but I've worked at it."

Soon after he became a boatman, Ken began fighting to save the rivers and canyons, always pushing for more wilderness. In 1963 a dam began to back the waters of Lake Powell over Glen Canyon, flooding what many considered to be the most beautiful gorge on the Colorado River.

"We could have saved Glen Canyon," Ken said, "but none of us knew how. We were just kids. They called it 'the place no one knew.' We knew it, but we couldn't do a thing. We didn't know how to fight the powers that be in those days."

I asked Ken where he would place the heart of the canyon country. "Glen Canyon," he answered without hesitation, "because we lost it."

Next morning, I load my pack, distributing the weight carefully. I don't want it to throw me off-balance. Reaching the rockslide, I study the possibilities. The best route crosses the bottom of the slide just above the lower cliff, but one stumble on the loose talus and it's over the edge. Higher up, the slope looks even worse.

As I begin crossing, I find tracks following the same route. Whoever crossed before took care not to trigger a new slide. Each person stepped in the footprints of the one before them. I do the same. Moving as smoothly and evenly as possible across the steep debris, I cover a long hundred yards. Reaching a solid ledge again, I look back at the rockslide, relieved to be seeing it from the far side.

A break in the cliff a half mile farther leads to the creek below. Pushing steadily down the canyon, I scramble around boulder jams and weave through tangles of Virginia creeper and sapling willow. A beaten path leads across a sand dune in the lower canyon. Blue sky spills through an immense perforation in the ridgeline dividing Stevens Canyon from the Escalante River. Recognizing the natural arch from previous trips, I find myself back in known country.

Boulders choke the tight throat of the canyon just beyond. I detour around the fill, stopping to rest beneath a petroglyph of a bighorn sheep. The bighorn are here, but the people who carved this one abandoned these canyons long ago.

Bushwhacking through a tamarisk thicket at the mouth of the canyon, I hear the rush of flowing water and moments later reach the Escalante River. On a map, its lower course twists like the root of a tree into Lake Powell a few miles below; its upper branches reach into the high Aquarius Plateau, 55 straight-line miles to the north. Survey parties under Major Powell put the Escalante on the map in the 1870s.

I wade downriver, probing for holes in the streambed with a beaver-cut stick, heading for a crack in the rock that leads to the rim country above. Ahead, the dark waters disappear around a bend, running deep within the rock mass. Lake Powell begins a few bends away. Part of the canyon country lies buried beneath its waters, but we carry the heart of it with us.

Flowers of the Mariposa lily burst with color near Capitol Reef's Bitter Creek Divide. Mariposas bloom in vermilion, orange, or yellow. The yellow are predominant at higher elevations.

Mormon pioneers settled Capitol Reef country in the 1880s. One of the earliest, Elijah C. Behunin, built a stone cabin in 1882 for his family of ten. Behunin's daughter Nettie became the first schoolteacher for the community—later called Fruita—where the Park Service has located its visitor center. Nettie taught eight grades in a one-room schoolhouse (opposite, top), now restored to its 1930s appearance. At recess, children played among Fremont cottonwoods below towering sandstone cliffs (opposite, bottom).

FOLLOWING PAGES: Apricot trees blossom near the Capitol Reef campground. Mormon homesteaders planted the first orchards, irrigating them from the nearby Fremont River. The pioneers sold apples, peaches, cherries, and apricots to other settlements.

Gypsum crystals called selenite (above) form Glass Mountain, an unusual mound of large crystals in Capitol Reef National Park's Lower Cathedral Valley. To the south, erosion has uncovered the sharply dipping beds of the Waterpocket Fold (opposite). The immense monocline, a single fold in the once level, now tilted layers of rock, forms the backbone of the park. Only a few streams breach the cliffs along the wall's hundred-mile length.

FOLLOWING PAGES: Rainwater in a sandstone pocket of Capitol Reef reflects the symmetry of flanking cliffs. The Powell Survey named the Waterpocket Fold after these natural basins.

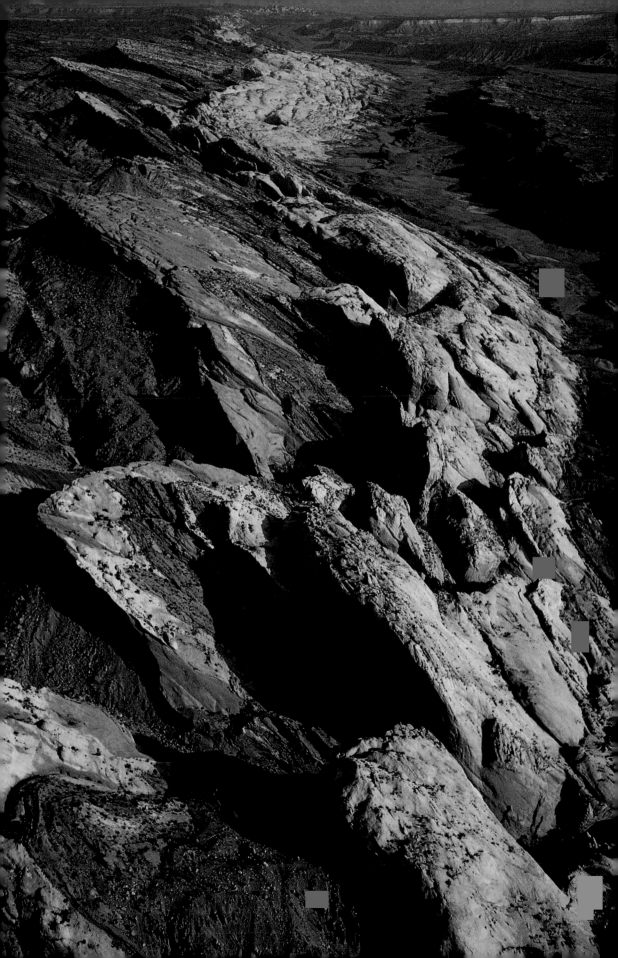

THE PEOPLE
OF THE
GREAT PLATEAU

Cliff Dwellings, Cowboys and Cornfields, Kachinas and Sacred Ceremonies

Night settles over a mesa-top village in northeastern Arizona far to the south of Navajo Mountain. Within the maze of stone houses and narrow streets, the tapered ends of a ladder angle through the smoke hole of a kiva. A Hopi priest waits inside the ceremonial chamber at the bottom of the ladder, his gray hair knotted at the back of his neck. Suddenly he hears the shaking of a rattle on the roof above and shouts a welcome to the spirits of his people. The kachinas have returned to Third Mesa.

Kachinas descend the ladder, one by one, crowding into the kiva as the cold air from outside spills off their bodies. Eyes bulge from snouted faces, eagle feathers fan out from heads, thick collars of juniper leaves circle their necks. Each kachina grips a gourd rattle in one hand and a painted bow in the other. The profusion of colors, the tang of juniper, the sounds of bells and rattles fill the kiva as kachinas continue climbing down the ladder.

The canyon Southwest takes its identity not only from the shape of the land but also from the people whose lives have been shaped by it—the Hopi and Zuni Indians, the Ute and Paiute, the Havasupai and Hualapai, the Navajo and Apache. Sometimes the match is so close the human landscape merges with the natural.

Ruins of the Anasazi, ancestors of modern Pueblo Indians, blend so smoothly with the bedrock it's hard to tell where one begins and the other ends. The cliff dwellings and great pueblos of this prehistoric people lie scattered throughout the

PRECEDING PAGES: Candlelight fills the ruins of Mesa Verde's Spruce Tree House in Colorado, reflecting the rich mix of southwestern cultures. At Christmas, park rangers illuminate the cliff dwelling with luminarias—Mexican paper-bag lanterns.

Fancy dancer spins in a swirl of colors as he keeps time to drumbeats. Indians from many tribes gather at powwows to compete for prizes awarded to those with the best traditional dance and the more exuberant fancy-dance styles.

Colorado Plateau, many in seven national parks and monuments. The indigenous peoples of the canyon country lead their lives within local horizons, their roots running deep in the place they live, their traditions recognizing the land as animate. "The land is alive," said Hopi tribal judge Delfred Leslie. "All living creatures come from the land. You treat the land like your mother—with respect, with reverence. Listen to your mother and in return your mother nurtures you, sustains your life."

All at once the kiva reverberates with a deep thumping beat so loud the enclosed air pulses, again and again. The drummer has called the dancers. Facing in one direction, the curving line of kachinas begins to dance, each step taken with rhythmic force. The kachinas chant in unison, their voices deep and hollow. They press forward with a focused intensity, whirl, and slowly return to where they began. Above the din of drum, rattle, and chant, priests cry out prayers of thanks.

During a break in the dancing, the kiva chief, a red scarf tied around his head, talks about the winter storms. "I wonder how those Navajo up there in snow country are doing," he says. Heavy snows have stranded many families, forcing the National Guard to fly in supplies. "They used to be able to take care of themselves when they had lots of horses. When it snowed, they could hitch up the wagon and go take care of the animals. Now everybody has a truck and can't go anywhere."

The dancing continues into the night as the shadows of the kachina gods move across the wall, bristling with feathers that shake with each beat of the drum. When the last dance has ended, the kachinas begin to leave. But a strong-voiced woman in the back calls out a command. The dancers hesitate, and a moment of uncertainty follows. The chief chuckles. "She says they have to dance until dawn."

The kachinas slowly re-form, expecting to dance for hours. But after completing another round, the woman lets them go. They scramble up the kiva ladder and disappear into the night.

Each year Hopi elders make a pilgrimage to national parks containing ruins they claim as ancestral villages—places like Canyon de Chelly, Mesa Verde, Betatakin, and Chaco Canyon. "They leave prayer feathers," says Delfred Leslie, "for the spirits of those still there."

Dressed in shorts and a Detroit Lions T-shirt, he sits on the porch of his father's house at First Mesa, near Third Mesa. "The ruins were never totally abandoned," Delfred says. "We refer to the ruins by name in each ceremony. They are mentioned to reconnect us to them, to tie them to the present."

His father, Ebin—a priest of the Flute Clan—sits patiently with a leader's solemn bearing, speaking only Hopi as his son interprets. Wearing a western shirt and a silver ring with the figure of a flute player cut into a silver overlay, Ebin says there are things he cannot talk about.

Often the Hopi elders choose to remain silent, even at the risk of having land important to them slip from their control. To disclose their fundamental attachment to these archaeological sites would break their vows of secrecy. "Knowledge can be given only through initiation," Delfred explains. "If you tell those not entitled to know, you break a covenant with yourself and other Hopi."

The Flute Clan priest confirms that during the clan migrations, the Hopi stopped for a time in many locations now within the national parks. These journeys were a spiritual search for the center of things—the place they now live. On the way they built pueblos and left their clan symbols carved and painted on the cliff walls.

The judge says the Hopi have found flute-player symbols throughout the canyon country as far north as Dinosaur National Monument. They also identify their ancestral stopping places, he says, by certain architectural features found in the ruins. "Everything has a reason for being where it is," he says; "everything has a purpose."

Zuni Indians, a Pueblo tribe in western New Mexico, share many traditions with the Hopi. Andrew Othole, cultural preservation coordinator for Zuni Pueblo, sits in his office at Black Rock. He says that the Zuni people split up when they emerged from the Fourth Underworld—some groups went north, some south. These migrations brought them to the sacred Middle Place where they now live. "These stories are in our Zuni folklore," he says. He pauses a moment before adding with a smile, "It's a different story than the archaeologists tell."

People lived at Zuni, 180 miles southeast of Navajo Mountain, in the 12th century when the Anasazi inhabited the great towns of Chaco Canyon farther north. People were still living there when the Spanish under Francisco Vásquez de Coronado entered the Southwest in 1540, searching for the legendary Seven Cities of Cíbola.

Congress approved plans to turn the Village of the Great Kivas and other ruined pueblos at Zuni into a national park in 1988, but the Zuni people rejected the idea. The park would have drawn tourists and created jobs, Andrew realizes, but it would have disrupted the life of the pueblo—both present and past. "People said it would disturb the spirits of our ancestors, the people still living in those ruins."

With National Park Service archaeologist Dabney Ford, I walk along the rim of Chaco Canyon in northwestern New Mexico. Above our heads, the sky is pulled thin by the distant horizons and pushed to enormous heights by climbing thunderheads. Surrounded by these vast open spaces, the Chaco Anasazi built a great ceremonial center between the cliffs of Chaco Canyon.

Pueblo Indians laid walls of fine stonework, course by course, into multistoried great houses containing hundreds of rooms. They engineered a network of roads linking Chaco Canyon to many of the 75 great-house communities in outlying areas. About A.D. 900 Chaco emerged as the center of the ancient Pueblo world, with its importance declining about 1150.

Dabney is wearing a gray and green Park Service *(Continued on page 140)*

Painted pottery signals a new direction for Navajo wares, traditionally coated with pitch and left unpainted. Influenced by sandpainting designs, this ceramic canteen depicts a careful balance between the sacred figures Sky Man and Earth Woman.

FOLLOWING PAGES: Navajo hogan stands where sky meets earth. Built facing east to catch the blessing of first light, the traditional Navajo home becomes a place to hold healing ceremonies. Its floor represents the earth; the ceiling symbolizes the sky.

Dancers in full regalia gather for a Navajo powwow in Window Rock, Arizona, 30 miles southeast of Canyon de Chelly. Powwow celebrations renew Indian pride through dancing, feasting, and rodeo events. Contest dancers wear elaborately decorated outfits when competing for prize money on the powwow circuit. A concha belt (opposite) circles the waist of a Navajo dancer. Such silver disks were originally inspired by Spanish spur buckles.

Near Canyon de Chelly, in Arizona, a herd of sheep and goats follows the leader back to the corral. Navajo often mix goats with their sheep, claiming the smarter goats make better leaders. Navajo cowboys (opposite) round up cattle for branding. Sheep, cows, and horses arrived in the Southwest with Spanish settlers in the 17th century. The Navajo soon became skilled horsemen, captured livestock, and started their own herds.

FOLLOWING PAGES: Spider Rock, in tradition the home of the Navajo deity Spider Woman, casts a thin shadow upon sandstone cliffs that drop 1,000 feet to the floor of Canyon de Chelly.

uniform offset by a pair of horned-lizard earrings. Together we reach the ruins of Pueblo Alto. The great house occupies a commanding position with a wide view of mesas and mountains held sacred by Navajo and Pueblo Indians. A dark curtain of rain falls in the distance. Rainfall averages about eight inches a year at Chaco, but even that small amount is erratic and undependable. Often the rains come too early or too late in the growing season.

"If you were a farmer trying to exist, you wouldn't pick this canyon," Dabney says. Winter temperatures drop to 20 degrees below zero and sometimes hit 40 below. "You'd go almost anywhere else. These people were farmers—everyone had to be. But there was also something else happening here."

Across the canyon from Pueblo Alto lies Casa Rinconada, a great kiva. Well-laid walls of shaped stone close in upon themselves in a circular chamber, 63 feet in diameter, sunk in the top of a knoll. Early Pueblo Indians used great kivas as centers of public assembly and ritual observance. But no kivas this size remain among the

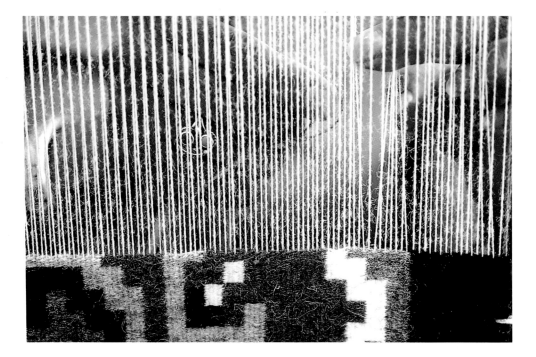

descendants of the people who lived here. What ceremonies they conducted within this chamber 900 years ago can only be guessed.

Pueblo Indians no longer perform rituals in the great kiva—though it is still sacred to them—but Anglos do. Rangers at Chaco Culture National Historical Park issue permits allowing groups with diverse beliefs, often labeled New Age, to hold ceremonies within the sites. For them, the park has become a source of spiritual strength. They leave offerings of crystals, feathers, and beads that park crews collect and turn over to the archaeologist. After cataloging them, curators store the offerings for future study—much the way they handle other artifacts.

Storm light illuminates an outcrop of cliffs against a cloud-dark sky to the north. Pale grass shimmers in the wind. "We're trying to decode the architecture,"

Dabney says. "The idea seemed pretty wild at first, but there's a real order to it."

With other archaeologists, Dabney has been surveying the layout of Chaco Canyon's core complex of great houses. Construction of the community may have been based on a precise design, astronomically oriented and tied to the wider landscape. "These buildings aren't randomly placed nor are they randomly oriented," she says. "We're finding a pattern, but we're not sure what it means. We're trying to understand the formula that was used to put these buildings together."

The purpose Pueblo Alto served has puzzled archaeologists for years. The great house, with more than 130 rooms, sheltered perhaps 25 to 50 people—a small population compared with those of other great houses. In the canyon below stand the ruins of Pueblo Bonito, excavated with National Geographic Society support in the 1920s. Stone walls, once standing five stories high, divide the village into 600 rooms with 40 kivas. A single, monumental edifice contained an entire town.

But what sets Pueblo Alto apart is its controlling position in the Chaco road

Spider Woman, says a Navajo legend, taught the people to weave. A Navajo weaver (opposite) works finely spun yarn into the intricate geometric design of a Two Gray Hills rug. Medicine men create equally complex images by carefully letting colored sand trickle through their fingers. Kneeling on a hogan floor, Chauncey Neboyia studies a sandpainting of Lightning Boy, one of the Navajo Holy People. At the end of a healing ceremony, medicine men scatter the sand in the wind.

system. Hundreds of miles of roadways radiate across the San Juan basin—a surprisingly elaborate system for a people without wheeled vehicles or pack animals. After negotiating the rough dirt road into the park, visitors might find it hard to believe that in the 11th and 12th centuries Chaco was the hub of the most sophisticated network of roads in North America.

Roadways, 30 feet wide and often curbed, knife straight across the blackbrush plains and badlands beyond Chaco. Road segments connect Chaco great houses to outlying pueblos and sources of raw materials. Some may run in a straight line for miles, then seemingly end in the middle of nowhere without having reached an obvious destination. Cardinal directions play an important role in modern Pueblo religion, leading some archaeologists to discount the practical aspect of these roads. The direction a road takes might have held a cosmological significance more important for the Anasazi than transportation or communication.

Walking along a low wall on the east side of Pueblo Alto, the park archaeologist reaches a gateway, three feet wide, where almost a dozen prehistoric roads once converged. Most roads are difficult to see from the ground, but a deep notch, plainly visible in a distant ridge, marks the passage of the longest of these — the Great North Road.

Disregarding terrain and flanked by roadside shrines and signal towers, the Great North Road takes a straight bearing for more than 30 miles to the rim of a canyon. The traceable roadway disappears at the remains of a wooden stairway descending into the eroded badlands. The Great North Road may have ended there, or it may have continued farther north to Salmon Ruin or Aztec Ruins.

T he layout of the ancient pueblo at Aztec Ruins National Monument resembles the architectural configuration of the main community in Chaco Canyon. Explorations by archaeologist Earl Morris for the American Museum of Natural History, beginning in 1916, revealed a complex of great houses, plazas, and great kivas. Rather than being an outpost of Chaco, Aztec may have become a major administrative and ritual center rivaling Chaco in scale. The Aztec center grew as the Chaco homeland began to lose its dominant position in the Anasazi world during the mid-1100s.

In the plaza of the ancient pueblo sits a restored great kiva, surrounded by cells of excavated room blocks, still and quiet. But all it takes is a shift in the wind to reanimate the old ruins. A breeze carries the distant voices of children playing, the low thump, thump, thump of a car stereo, the sharp bark of a dog. Sounds of the living rush in to fill the space left empty by the departure of the Anasazi centuries ago.

A Navajo woman living north of Chaco once told her grandson a story about the departure of the Anasazi. "She told me that a cloud of mist covered everything," says silversmith Lyle Yazzie. "When it lifted, everybody had disappeared."

Archaeologist Gwinn Vivian sees the abandonment of the Chaco basin differently. Wearing a silver Indian bracelet on his wrist, he sits in his office at the Arizona State Museum in Tucson.

"I think what ultimately happened," he says, "was that the size of the population simply exceeded the amount of food the people could grow. Once this happened, they were on the edge. Another major dry period came in, and that's what did them in. They just simply couldn't make it any longer. And the ultimate solution, which always seemed to be the Anasazi solution, was to move."

Gwinn grew up at Chaco Canyon, where his father directed excavations for years. Later he conducted his own digs there. "The Anasazi didn't disappear," he says. "They are still with us. The Chacoan people are sitting in the Rio Grande Valley today. The Anasazi didn't fail — they adapted. To some extent they mismanaged resources, but they were no different than we are today. And we're doing it on an enormous scale — and we know what we're doing. We should be learning from the past."

Mesa Verde, the second major center of Anasazi culture, lies north of Chaco Canyon, more than 130 miles east of Navajo Mountain. The contrast between the two settings is striking: At Chaco a barren canyon juts through a stark plain; at Mesa Verde clouds scrape along the evergreen rim of a tableland perched 2,000 feet above the valley.

In December 1888 two cowboys followed an Indian trail up Mesa Verde searching for stray cattle. Once on top, Richard Wetherill and Charlie Mason trailed through thick stands of piñon and juniper along the edge of a canyon. They paused to rest their horses as snow flurries swept over the mesa top. Looking across the canyon through the falling snow, they spotted the vague shapes of a "magnificent city" perched on the cliffside. What they saw was a ruined village clustered about a round tower that rose three stories—all sheltered in a pocket of the overhanging rock. Wetherill named it Cliff Palace.

A Ute Indian had told Wetherill about these ruins, warning him not to enter them and disturb the spirits of the dead. But the cowpunchers lashed together a log ladder with their lariats and descended into the canyon. Reaching the cliff dwelling, they scrambled over mounds of rubble and entered an intact room. Inside they found a cooking pot resting on the hearth and food bowls sitting on the floor—as if the Anasazi had left everything in place, expecting to return.

At Mesa Verde National Park the past becomes visible. The cliff-house formation shelters nearly 600 dwellings, so well preserved that some rooms still retain coats of plaster painted with geometric designs. A jar, now displayed in the park museum, was found with more than 31 pounds of corn kernels and a single black pebble sealed inside it. Another exhibit holds a pair of child-size crutches, padded in the crooks, left behind 700 years ago.

Most cliff dwellings contain fewer than 5 rooms, but Cliff Palace—the largest cliff dwelling in North America—has 240 rooms and kivas. In the 1200s it housed a population of perhaps 250, but below, in Montezuma Valley, archaeologists are excavating towns from the same time period large enough to hold many more people.

"We now realize that the Mesa Verde communities were much smaller than others nearby," says Bruce Bradley, an archaeologist with the Crow Canyon Archaeological Center near Cortez. "The main reason for the focus on the ruins at Mesa Verde has been their degree of preservation, not that they represent the center of Anasazi occupation of the region." With partial support from the National Geographic Society, Bradley is excavating Sand Canyon Pueblo, an Anasazi town of at least 420 rooms, 90 kivas, and 14 towers enclosed within an outer wall. "The population centers were down in the valley in places like Sand Canyon," he says. "Mesa Verde was the suburbs. We're digging downtown."

The abandonment of Sand Canyon was an exception to the planned departure of people from other sites. It happened suddenly. Kivas on one side of the pueblo were all burned. Bodies lay where they fell with their skulls crushed. What happened may never be known—possibly an attack by outsiders, perhaps strife among the Anasazi villages. All we know is that the people left their dead unburied and never returned. "It was," Bradley says, "a traumatic abandonment."

The archaeologist leaves his office to meet a busload of Zuni students arriving at the center for a five-day field program. As the students crowd downstairs for a demonstration of stone-tool making, a teacher stops a Zuni boy. Holding him by the shoulders, the teacher looks him in the eye. "Your great-great-great-grandmother came from here," he tells the student, who nods his head, anxious to join his friends.

In the hallway nearby, Jim Colleran pauses a moment in front of a ceramic bowl excavated at Sand Canyon. He leads field programs (Continued on page 147)

In Hopi life, corn is sacred. It is also a
staple food. Beginning in the spring, the
Hopi plant drought-resistant varieties.
Later in the season, a Hopi farmer
(above) tends his cornfield as drying

winds shake the stalks. A kachina doll (opposite, lower), with an ear of corn, represents Hahaiwuhti, a mother of Hopi kachinas, or supernatural beings. A young Hopi woman (opposite, upper) wears her hair in the whorls that traditionally identify a girl eligible for marriage. She holds a perfect ear, called Mother Corn, which can be used to bless a newborn child.

for the center on ancient southwestern cultures. Admiring the intricate black-on-white design decorating the piece, he points out holes drilled on each side of a crack where it had been mended when still in use.

"I will tell you a story about that," he says with the trace of an Irish lilt. "When I grew up in the west of Ireland, we had a great china closet. The large, valuable pieces were kept on top. Nine times out of ten they had been drilled and fixed by the blacksmith. It's an interesting sort of tradition—the same as the Anasazi."

Broken pottery paves the surface of a large mound on a bank of the Mancos River within the Ute Mountain Tribal Park. Running full from recent rains, the river skirts the foot of Mesa Verde. The tribal park lies adjacent to Mesa Verde National Park and contains hundreds of Anasazi surface ruins and cliff dwellings. Bold, red Ute pictographs and prehistoric petroglyphs cover cliff walls along the river.

Tommy May, Ute tribal guide, picks up a potsherd with a fingerprint pressed into the clay centuries ago. Wearing a T-shirt with a faded flute-player logo, he ambles over the site finding items of interest to show a handful of tourists he escorts—a finely worked arrowhead of red chert, a piece of shell bracelet traded from the Pacific coast. A visitor, he says, once asked him if he was an Anasazi. " 'Yes,' I teased her, 'I am the last of the Anasazi. I live way up there in that cliff dwelling.' "

The joking ends when Tommy crosses an arroyo and notices human bone eroding from a bank. He tells about a Ute who stayed overnight in the canyon. The Indian saw a man building a stone wall in a ruin, but the apparition disappeared when he approached. "I believe there's spirits among this canyon," Tommy says.

Returning to the truck, Tommy takes his party higher into Mancos Canyon. Driving slowly, he points to a pictograph on a nearby cliff of a sunburst with a red handprint next to it. Jack House, the last traditional chief of the Ute Mountain people, painted much of the canyon's Ute rock art in the first half of this century. Tommy says the people called Chief Jack House by his nickname, Hand-in-Sun. "That's his signature," he says, looking up at the red-painted sun.

Tommy tells those near him a legend about Sleeping Ute Mountain—a landmark seen from throughout the Four Corners country, rising across the valley from Mesa Verde. He says the main peak is the elbow of a wounded warrior lying down to rest. "One day, they say, the warrior will rise up to help the Ute people."

The trail to Keet Seel in Navajo National Monument enters the storm-cut Navajo sandstone. Cliffs close in and the stepped canyon profile gives way to sheer slickrock walls. In the late 1200s Tsegi Canyon became an important center of the Kayenta Anasazi, the third major branch of the Anasazi people.

The outside world has known about Keet Seel for less than a century. In horseback days, the search for stray livestock often took explorers into places they might never have thought of going. A stray cow led Richard Wetherill to Cliff Palace; a stray mule led him to Keet Seel in 1895.

"Richard Wetherill lost a mule," says archaeologist Marietta Davenport, "and found Keet Seel." She is the great-granddaughter of John Wetherill, Richard's

His face sprinkled with corn pollen and painted with red marks representing rain, a dancer exemplifies the Hopi belief that rainfall combines with the earth to produce life-giving corn. His turquoise necklace symbolizes the blue of water and sky.

brother and fellow guide, ruins explorer, and Indian trader. In 1909 John Wetherill guided an archaeological exploring party into Tsegi Canyon. Led up a side canyon by a local Navajo, they discovered Betatakin, a 140-room cliff dwelling. In the same year Wetherill became the first custodian of Navajo National Monument—at an annual salary of $12.

A Navajo guide brings up the rear of a mounted party of tourists on their way to Keet Seel. A sign next to a tributary of Laguna Creek warns, "Flash flood and quicksand, take upper trail." The horses climb a sandy terrace, following the trail through groves of Gambel oak and box elder that scatter the overhead sun into fragments of light. As the trees thin, the air fills with the sharp aroma of sagebrush—its flannel-soft leaves still wet from recent showers.

Descending the trail, the horses splash across the creek and clomp up the far bank to a grassy bench. Smooth cliff rock drops from the rim in a long, incurving wall streaked with desert varnish. Seen from the strip of green on the canyon floor, the immense red-rock cliffs squeeze the sky into a narrow band of blue.

Park ranger Russell Whitla puts on his flat-brimmed campaign hat as he steps outside his cabin. He says hello to the new arrivals and leads them up the foot trail to Keet Seel. The trail bends toward a massive alcove sheltering the cliff dwelling. For a moment, the ruins blend with the canyon walls. But then the dark rectangular entryways emerge from the rock matrix, followed by the flat planes of wall and roof.

At a vantage point on the trail, the ranger stops for a minute without saying a word, letting the place speak for itself. The ancient village clings to a ledge sunk deep within the overhanging cliff. Centuries have swept it clean of the debris of daily life, the jumble of human loves and hates. What remain are the empty rooms of a human community embedded in the natural world.

The party climbs a wooden ladder into the deserted village of more than 150 interconnected rooms and kivas crowded onto a broad shelf of sandstone. The cliff falls away on one side; the canyon wall flares overhead on the other. Walls of laid stone and mud-coated, woven sticks meet at right angles, enclosing every square foot of the ledge. Terraced houses, built without trowel or level, cluster together as flat-topped as the mesa country beyond the canyon. Bedrock serves as foundation, back wall, and roof, blurring the line between geology and architecture.

Among the pictographs painted on the back wall of the rock shelter lies a flute player. The figure reclines on its back, one leg crossed over the other, passing away the centuries playing a tune no longer heard.

Standing among the ruins, Russell Whitla says that in the last half of the 13th century, 700 Kayenta Anasazi lived in the canyon, perhaps 150 of those at Keet Seel. But a cycle of arroyo cutting destroyed the Anasazi fields, washing away much of the canyon's alluvial fill and lowering the water table. A generation after moving into the canyon, the Anasazi sealed the doorways of their houses and left.

"I came here nine years ago for a summer," Russell says, "and have been here ever since."

As the group leaves the cliff dwelling, the ranger points out how the natural alcove faces southeast. That lets the pueblo catch the low-angled winter sunlight, while the overhanging rock shades it from the high summer sun. But the Anasazi link with geological features went beyond the practical.

Far to the south of Keet Seel, crews under Park Service archaeologist Bruce Anderson spent seven years crisscrossing the high desert grasslands of Wupatki National Monument. The surface ruins of Wupatki lie on the southwestern edge of the Anasazi country. The survey located artifacts ranging from an 11,000-year-old Clovis spearpoint to a loaded .44 Colt Peacemaker—"probably lost by a cowboy on his way home who was mad as hell when he found it missing," says Anderson.

Most of the thousands of archaeological sites were connected with the pre-historic Pueblo Indians. Anderson found a close link between Anasazi house sites and unusual geological features—earth cracks, blowholes, and rock outcrops.

Earth cracks break the surface of the park, leading into an extensive system of underground fissures usually too narrow to enter. Connected with the underground system, blowholes act as a natural barometer. Air rushes out at speeds up to 35 miles per hour when the atmospheric pressure is low; the flow of air reverses when the air pressure is high. Navajo and Hopi continue to visit blowholes at Wupatki, leaving ritual offerings of prayer feathers and small bundles of plants.

"The prehistoric inhabitants," Anderson says, "were really fascinated by geologic features. They liked to locate around them. They were attuned to them. You see it over and over again at Wupatki."

N avajo guide Chauncey Neboyia stands on the brink of Canyon de Chelly looking across at Spider Rock. The solitary pinnacle splits into two spires, the higher reaching 800 feet above the canyon floor. "Spider Rock," Chauncey says slowly, listening to the sound of the name. He speaks English in a gentle voice with a Navajo cadence, wears faded jeans, and has a gray stubble on his chin. Several turkey buzzards hang in the air, their wings tipping in half turns as they scan the ground. "It's the most sacred part of the canyon," Chauncey says. "Medicine men say their prayers here in the spring when the first grass comes up."

Canyon de Chelly, 95 miles southeast of Navajo Mountain, branches into three major prongs—del Muerto, de Chelly, and Monument Canyon. Snowmelt and storm runoff have carved a course through the sandstone as sinuous as a raindrop running down a windowpane.

The word "canyon" is applied to a wide range of sunken terrain—from an amphitheater to a narrow cleft, from a cliff-lined wash to a vast system of interlocking gorges. But Canyon de Chelly is a classic canyon—high perpendicular walls falling sheer to a sandy, stream-cut floor. The proportions of rock and sky stay true, and even the human presence fits—a few hogans, fields where the canyon widens, and a dirt track winding along the canyon bottom.

The old guide looks across the deep vista at the narrow summit of Spider Rock. "They say Spider Woman used to live on top of Spider Rock," he says. "Every morning when she gets up, she prays for a rainbow. Spider Woman travels on the rainbow; she goes over to the other side." The spire rises almost half again as high as the Washington Monument, enclosed within canyon walls even higher.

"Spider Woman is the holiest person," he continues. "They say Spider Woman made twelve gods. One god for the earth, one god for the sky, the moon, sun, and stars, and all these plants and animals, humans, and rains."

As a young man, Chauncey had worked with archaeologist Earl Morris, excavating cliff dwellings in the canyon. Guided by John Wetherill in 1922, Morris made his first trip into Canyon de Chelly. *(Continued on page 156)*

Generations of Pueblo Indians have maintained their traditions in New Mexico villages along the Rio Grande. An elder of Santa Clara Pueblo (opposite) makes his way to the plaza for a winter dance that seeks to ensure an abundance of game and to propitiate slain animals' spirits. Multistoried Taos Pueblo steps skyward, preserving an age-old sense of community with nature. Bread for a feast bakes in an adobe oven at Santa Clara.

FOLLOWING PAGES: Kilted dancer grips a rattle and a lightning prayer stick, tipped with downy eagle feathers, during a Buffalo Dance at Santa Clara Pueblo. Evergreen sprigs and lightning represent aspects of the life-giving rains.

Near Ganado, Arizona, handwoven Navajo rugs flood Hubbell Trading Post with colors and patterns as bold as the natural surroundings. Now a national historic site, the trading post has operated on the Navajo reservation for more than a century. Trader Bill Malone stands with his wife, Minnie, next to the wooden counter where he conducts business with local Indians and visitors. Malone carries on the tradition of hospitality set by post founder John Lorenzo Hubbell, who began trading with the Navajo in the 1870s.

Pioneer skills have stayed in fashion at Pipe Spring National Monument, where ranger Yvonne Heaton stitches a Double Wedding Ring quilt. Pipe Spring, one of the few reliable water sources in a region known as the Arizona Strip, north of the Grand Canyon, became a center of cattle ranching in the late 1800s. Mormon settlers built a stone fort called Winsor Castle to guard the springs and to protect their cattle against Indian raids. Inside the fort, a portrait of Mormon leader Brigham Young hangs above the fireplace in a simply furnished parlor (opposite), where settlers gathered in the evenings to read and sing.

The next year he began excavating Mummy Cave, where he uncovered the naturally desiccated mummy of a Pueblo Indian who had lived before the Anasazi had pottery or the bow and arrow. A basket covered his face; he held a spear thrower in his right hand; and a flute lay on his chest.

A rectangular tower, three stories high, stands on a ledge joining the twin alcoves of Mummy Cave. Two rows of vigas—log rafters—cast a hatching of shadows across the face of the tower. Clearing debris from inside the tower, the archaeologists found a series of prayer sticks placed in the wall identical to ones found in the same location in a Mesa Verde cliff dwelling.

Built in A.D. 1284, Tower House may have been the last Anasazi building constructed in Canyon de Chelly. The canyon dwellers had abandoned the region by 1300. But potsherds indicate Pueblo people occasionally returned over the centuries until the Navajo put down permanent roots here in the 18th century.

Before leaving Spider Rock, Chauncey talks about the chants sung during healing ceremonies. He once practiced as a medicine man himself. "The Holy People learn these songs by listening to the echoes." He pauses for a moment as if he's listening for something, but the only sound is a trace of wind rising from below. "Not many echoes these days," he says, turning away from the rim.

A painting of Spider Rock by the artist Louis Akin hangs in the home of legendary Navajo trader John Lorenzo Hubbell. His house is now part of the Hubbell Trading Post National Historic Site, 35 miles south of Canyon de Chelly.

Navajo rugs cover the floor, the bold Ganado reds woven into geometric patterns of gray, black, and white. Paintings by western artists, such as J. J. Mora, John Warner Norton, and Maynard Dixon, and portraits of American Indians, oils of canyon landscapes, and paintings of Hopi ceremonies crowd the room.

"The paintings at Hubbell are the largest collection of artwork held by the National Park Service," says Ed Chamberlin, a former Park Service curator.

Founded by John Lorenzo Hubbell in 1878, Hubbell Trading Post is one of the last traditional posts still operating. Inside the stone building, harnesses hang from wooden beams, a saddle rests on a potbellied stove in the middle of the plank floor, cases of soda pop lie stacked in front of the counter.

Bill Malone, trader at Hubbell for 11 years, says many Navajo like the traditional posts and travel long distances to do business at them. "But," he adds, "they are dying out." Only a few still trade over the counter like Hubbell. "The others have been sold, changed to convenience stores, vandalized, burned out."

Leaning against the counter, his gray sideburns cut long, Bill talks about the Navajo country, his home for most of his life. He stops for a moment to joke in Navajo with a customer, then tells me that he's married to a Navajo woman.

"Once my daughter got sick," he says. "My wife wanted to take her to the doctor. I said sure, take her to the hospital. Three or four days later my daughter was better. 'See what Anglo doctors can do for you?' I told my wife. She looked at me and said, 'I took her to the medicine woman.' "

Malone has encouraged a revival of the old styles of weaving. Paintings of designs used by Hubbell hang in the rug room of the post. "Many times people see an old rug painting and want one like it," says Malone, "so I find a weaver to do it."

An old Navajo woman drove down from Canyon de Chelly to sell a weaving. Malone inspects her rug, smoothing it out on the floor. "It isn't perfect," he says, "but she came all that way. I'll buy rugs that aren't perfect from young ones and old ones. They're either just learning or they're still trying."

The oldest sample of Navajo weaving came from Massacre Cave, less than a mile from Mummy Cave. David Wilson, wearing a vest over his T-shirt, stands on a point overlooking the cave. Head of the Canyon de Chelly guides association, David grew up in the canyon below, herding sheep for his grandparents and growing beans, corn, and cantaloupe in the nearby fields. He remembers life there before the early 1960s, when people used horse-drawn wagons, not trucks. About 20 Navajo families, he says, still live seasonally in Canyon de Chelly.

Looking down at the place where the massacre happened, David tells the story. Spanish soldiers under Lt. Antonio Narbona rode into the canyon in 1805. More than a hundred Navajo women, children, and old men climbed to a ledge hidden under a shallow overhang high above the canyon floor. The soldiers rode past without seeing them. David says a woman, angry with the leaders of the band for not allowing her to marry her cousin, tried to reveal their position.

"One of the other ladies," he says, "jump up and grab her to pull her down. But both of them fell off. When she screamed, that's when the Spanish looked back. That's when they turned around." Unable to shoot into the cave from below, Narbona sent riflemen to the rim. "They shoot them with the ricochets," David says. Only one old man survived to tell the tale.

Despite this tragedy, the canyon remained an Indian refuge for another 60 years. Determined to defeat the Navajo, Gen. James Carleton ordered former scout and mountain man Kit Carson to undertake a scorched earth campaign against them. Colonel Carson led a force of New Mexico troops and Ute Indians to this Navajo stronghold, intending to bring about their total surrender.

"Kit Carson and his troops came here," David continues, describing the events of 1864. "They burn all the hogans they see here, and they kill lots of livestock, and they chop down all the peach orchards. It was in the wintertime. Lots of people froze and lots of people starved. So finally they give up."

More than a century later, the scorched earth policy against the Navajo remains a bitter memory. In 1984 Bill Johnson, a retired fighter pilot teaching high school in Colorado, came to the reservation looking for a useful project for his students. A Navajo woman told him they could replant her orchard—the one Kit Carson cut down. "Cutting the peach trees," Bill says, "was to them an incomprehensible act."

With his students, he began to plant peach trees. He planted so many that a Navajo friend began calling him Billy Peachpit. The project, Trees for Mother Earth, became so successful, Johnson now plants full-time, working with many school groups. Eventually, he says, the Navajo on his staff will take over from him.

Kit Carson's soldiers cut thousands of trees; Johnson and his students have replanted about 9,000. But over the years the reason for planting the fruit trees has changed. Wilson Hunter, a Navajo who grew up at Canyon de Chelly, guided Johnson on his first trip into the canyon. Wilson is now a park ranger in charge of interpretation for Canyon de Chelly National Monument. "People have come up to me," he says, "saying they are sorry for what their people did. That's not the point. You can't

Cowboys move Redd Ranch cattle out of the La Sal Mountains before the winter snows. Rancher Hardy Redd's family arrived in southeastern Utah with a wagon train of Mormon colonists who completed an epic crossing of Glen Canyon in 1880.

dwell on the past. The peach trees are good—not as a remembrance of the past but as tools to provide a future for all."

The National Park Service protects and interprets the archaeological sites in the canyon on land owned by the Navajo tribe. Sitting behind the visitor center at the mouth of the canyon, Wilson tells me that balance is the key to proper management.

"We're trying to balance two different worlds," says the 1991 recipient of the Freeman Tilden Award, one of the Park Service's top honors. "We're helping the local Navajo people, making them part of the park. And we are interpreting our culture, we are interpreting ourselves, to non-Indians."

As he gets up to leave, Wilson adds, "Canyon de Chelly goes beyond being a place of beauty. It's more personal. It has special significance. It's alive."

Peach trees, not yet in bloom, grow on the floor of the canyon. Nearby stands a notched-log hogan with prickly pear cactus growing on the dirt roof. With the help of her grandchildren, a Navajo woman burns tumbleweeds as a small herd of goats and sheep grazes nearby.

In the cliff above, archaeoastronomer Von Del Chamberlain stands within a deep sandstone pocket called Deadman Cave. His wide-brimmed hat tilts back as he studies the domed ceiling of the cave. A field of painted stars curves high overhead.

"Doesn't this feel like a planetarium?" asks Von Del, the director of the Hansen Planetarium in Salt Lake City. He is speaking to a group from the Canyonlands Field Institute on a tour of Canyon de Chelly. "I feel like giving a lecture," he jokes.

Volcanic eruptions, beginning in A.D. 1065, buried the homes of Sinagua farmers, ancestors of the Hopi Indians. Legends describe a firestorm of molten embers forming the red-hued cone now in Arizona's Sunset Crater Volcano National Monument.

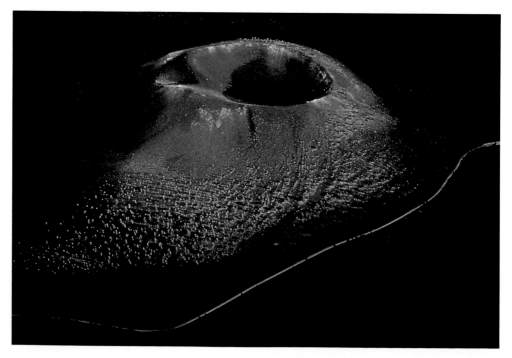

For years he has been studying Navajo star ceilings, having recorded about 70 of them—many in this canyon.

The Navajo used a four-pointed cross symbol, often painted in black or red, to represent a star. Chauncey Neboyia said they used to attach crossed strips of yucca to the end of an arrow and shoot it against the ceiling of an overhanging rock to make the mark.

Von Del has studied Navajo star lore and the depiction of common constellations in sandpaintings and on ritual objects. But he doesn't find these patterns represented in the star ceilings. He believes another explanation is likely. The archaeoastronomer often finds the stars placed on cracked ceilings, threatening to fall, over Anasazi ruins, or over areas used by the Navajo and their animals. Star ceilings, he says, may be for protection against the danger of falling rock.

In the mid-1980s a medicine man traveled into the canyon with the park superintendent. "He told the superintendent," Von Del says, "that the stars hold the sky together, and those up there hold the rock together."

Inside Deadman Cave, Von Del unwraps a long wooden flute inlaid with stars. He stands in the circular mouth of the cave and begins to play. Blowing into the flute, he fills the cave with a string of haunting notes, deep and resonating. The tune draws a white-throated swift into the cave to investigate, chirping as it turns and darts back into the open. As the song ends, the last note echoes off the far wall of the canyon.

At Bandelier National Monument, New Mexico, candles burn in chambers carved by prehistoric villagers in cliffs of compressed volcanic ash, or tuff. On summer nights, visitors assemble below the cliff dwellings, as a Pueblo elder chants traditional songs.

An archaeologist instructs students at Crow Canyon Archaeological Center, Colorado, in the value of careful observation as they sift dirt excavated from a prehistoric site. Another group (opposite) uses whisk brooms and trowels to gently uncover clues to the ancient Anasazi ways of life. Working in this valley below Mesa Verde, archaeologists investigate why a people who lived in the Four Corners area for 14 centuries abandoned their homeland by A.D. 1300. The answer may wait for some of these apprentices.

Visitors to Chaco Culture National Historical Park, New Mexico, pause within the ruins of Pueblo Bonito. In the 12th century the village contained hundreds of rooms stacked in five tiers above two great kivas. To the north, at Aztec Ruins National Monument, daylight filters into the only restored great kiva in the Southwest. The circular chamber served as the ceremonial focus for this Anasazi community.

FOLLOWING PAGES: Stars circle above the curving walls of Casa Rinconada, the ruins of a great kiva within Chaco Canyon. Anasazi Indians may have marked the longest day of the year by watching a shaft of light enter the chamber on the summer solstice and strike a niche on the far wall.

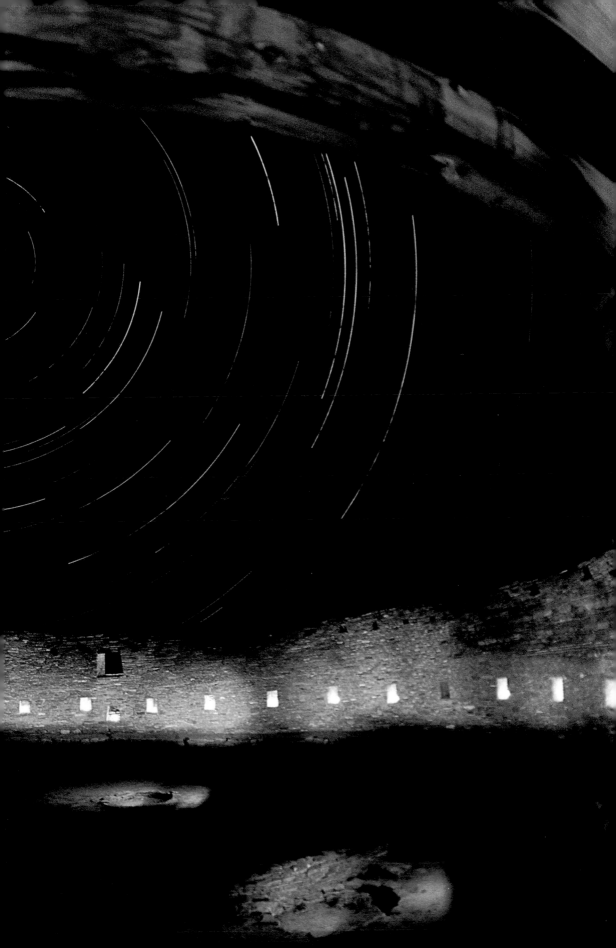

GRAND CANYON

Living Abyss of the Ages, an Open Book of Earth's History

Night fills the empty space below, concealing all but a dim outline of canyon rim and falling cliff. Up early, I stand on the edge of a narrow promontory known as Cape Solitude North. Straight ahead lies the Grand Canyon, sunk in the hollow darkness.

Far from the nearest Navajo camp, even farther from a paved road, the only break in the dark expanse is a point of light on the South Rim 12 miles away. It flickers in the emptiness like a spark drifting in the night sky. The only sound is the rush of waters flowing toward the confluence of the Little Colorado and Colorado Rivers, three-quarters of a mile below.

As dawn nears, I begin packing my gear. Storm clouds that moved in during the night have spread overhead, edged in light. Below, the cliff walls begin to emerge from the flat backdrop. My friend Dave Hellod wakes up and loads his pack, getting ready for our hike down to the confluence.

Suddenly an infusion of color fills the air with a soft red haze. The sky turns incandescent. A mist of pure light, suspended, without motion, envelops me. The moment is so unexpected, I stop everything, taken by its strange beauty.

The sun tops the horizon, clearing the air. The canyon deepens and draws back into distant alcoves, revealing cliffs and the ruins of cliffs. A band of sunlight strikes across the North Rim, leaving the lower ravines in gray halftones. A rainbow arches above in laminations of brilliant green, yellow, and red that disappear

PRECEDING PAGES: "A gigantic statement for even nature to make, all in one mighty stone word," wilderness-lover John Muir said of the Grand Canyon. From Yaki Point on the South Rim the great gorge gapes more than 15 miles across.

Oars dig into waves as Jeff Schloss battles rock-strewn Hance Rapid. Today thousands challenge the Colorado River, first run in 1869 by John Wesley Powell. "The boat . . . leaps and bounds," he wrote, "like a thing of life."

into the dark clouds above and reappear beyond Point Imperial nine miles away.

"Amazing," Dave says, looking around. Working as an outdoor instructor to put himself through college, he left everything on the spur of the moment for a chance to see this place for the first time. "This is so great."

Marble Canyon drops away on one side of us and, on the other, the gorge of the Little Colorado. Before us stands the entrance to the Grand Canyon, the sometimes mile-deep section of an immense canyon system linked by the Colorado River. The river runs for 277 miles through a continuous gorge from Lees Ferry to the Grand Wash Cliffs. The final 215 miles lie within the Grand Canyon labyrinth—a great repository of solitude as well as a place visited each year by millions.

Earlier I had stood on a viewpoint near Grand Canyon Village, on the South Rim. So many others had stood in the same spot their feet had worn the bedrock smooth. But a vast canyon opened below, so remote in parts that people have disappeared there without a trace. Most of the nearly five million people who yearly travel to the Grand Canyon see it from the South Rim.

On this trip I've decided to approach it from a different angle. I'll begin here at the head of the Grand Canyon and finish where it ends in the western gorge. From our promontory I look directly down the passageway carved by the Colorado. Where the Little Colorado enters the great river from the east, Maj. John Wesley Powell camped on his first exploration in 1869. The night before entering the Grand Canyon, he contemplated what lay before him. "We have an unknown distance yet to run," he wrote, "an unknown river to explore."

In three months, Powell and his crew traveled a thousand miles down the Colorado through a string of unmapped canyons. Facing constant hard work and frequent danger, they never knew what lay around the next bend. After weeks of uncertainty, the not knowing began to work on them, taking on mythic proportions. The unexplored canyons carved by this hidden river became Powell's "Great Unknown."

Dave and I park our truck near a narrow slot in the rim. I remember the route below as being steep and difficult. We'll have to push hard to get to the confluence and back in one day. We ease down a rocky slope. Rain begins as we descend a series of short cliffs, leaving a rope tied above the most difficult pitch for the return climb. At the bottom of the slot we traverse a narrow ledge to a high-angled slope. A

Algae streak crystalline Havasu Creek, spilling over dams of travertine formed by deposits of calcium carbonate. Silt-laden in full spate, the Little Colorado River (opposite) plunges 185 feet over this tributary's Grand Falls. Whether as snowmelt, raindrops, gentle cascades, or explosive flash floods, water played a major role in the creation of the Grand Canyon and continues to shape its rugged landscape today.

mix of shattered rock spills down the headwall of a short canyon leading to the Little Colorado. We pick our way lower, reaching the river two and a half hours later. Floodwaters roll muddy red through the deep gorge with a low, swallowed roar.

Leaving our packs to explore up the river, we soon spot a man standing alone among the rocks. He wears headphones draped around his neck and jots notes on a clipboard. Bob Reed, a researcher at Arizona State University, tells us he's conducting a study of Grand Canyon rattlesnake behavior. He's been tracking one of his seven snakes by means of a surgically implanted radio transmitter.

"There she is," Bob says, sticking a thermometer in the ground next to a rocky ledge. It takes a second glance for me to spot the rattlesnake, tucked under the outcrop and blending with the rock. The female rattler in front of us had given birth that spring, he says. I ask if the babies are still with her. "No," he says, "with rattlesnakes there's no parental nurturing."

Dave and I turn down the Little Colorado. Not far from the confluence we meet Paul Marsh and John Cook cleaning a fishnet stretched beneath a rock overhang. They're part of a team from Arizona State and the Navajo Natural Heritage Program, who are conducting a four-year study of the endangered humpback chub and other native fish. Scientists thought the chub entered the Little Colorado only to spawn, but Paul's team has learned that many live in the river year-round. On some days the team captures hundreds of fish, tagging them before releasing them back into the water.

Wearing a rain parka, John wades waist deep in the muddy water, returning with a net containing two hand-size chub. The immature fish shine with a silvery iridescence but haven't developed the hump of the adults. "The fine for intentionally catching one of these without a permit," John says, "runs as high as $50,000."

Rounding a point, Dave and I reach the place where the waters meet. Muddy currents from each river flow side by side until they gradually fold into each other to become a single river. We duck under a ledge to get out of the rain and eat lunch. A lone raven perches on a rock and waits for us to leave before checking for scraps.

Each time I enter this canyon it's a different place. The shifting weather and light rework the face of the Grand Canyon moment by moment. An entire season's weather can flash past in a single day. *(Continued on page 179)*

FOLLOWING PAGES: Sunset and clouds do-si-do beyond Mather Point, one of the most frequented canyon overlooks. "The clouds are children of the heavens," wrote Powell, "and when they play among the rocks they lift them to the region above." Light catches a butte called Isis Temple, after the Egyptian goddess. Early on, a tradition began of naming canyon splendors for deities and ancient architectural wonders.

176

Scallops of travertine provide precarious footing for hikers below Havasu Falls. Spring-fed Havasu Creek tumbles over three main waterfalls on its way to the Colorado, and creates a verdant canyon oasis for Indians called

Havasupai—"people of the blue-green water"—who, for some seven centuries, have made their home there.

The raven has only a short wait before we begin our return trek to the rim. A drenching rain falls as we walk up the Little Colorado under the path of the storm. Thunder rolls across the rimlands, echoing through the gorge. Clouds drift overhead as runoff threads down the rock walls. Dave reaches out his hands, palms up, to catch the rain. "The canyon's alive," he says with a smile, his blond hair plastered wet against his neck.

Reaching the foot of the route, we begin the long ascent. Heavy clouds tumble over the brink, spilling down the ravines and hiding the notch that leads out. A few sharp angles of the rock wall above cut through the cloud cover. The rest lies hidden. Somewhere on the cliff before us a rock breaks loose with a boom and crashes below. We hear it fall but don't see it.

Working our way higher, we get hit by a burst of hail followed moments later by a flood of sunlight, and then by a wind-driven cloud sweeping over us as it flies up the canyon wall. The only reminder that we're still in a desert is a green barrel cactus growing on a rocky shelf and bristling with red needles.

Nearing the rim slot, Dave and I hear the high, thin sound of moving water. I check the ravine ahead, but only a trickle flows from it. Suddenly a flash flood shoots over the near rim and falls hundreds of feet to the broken slope below. Having reached a point above it, we're in no danger and continue climbing.

Once in the narrow chute beyond, we scale the final cliffs with water running down our arms as we grab handholds. After retrieving the rope, we reach the truck, bone tired but feeling good.

But with 20 miles of flooded desert to cross we can't relax yet. The daylong rains have saturated the ground. Ruts in the road have turned into flooded ditches, and standing water covers the low spots of the desert. Keeping our momentum up, I aim the truck across the sagebrush expanse, often abandoning the muddy track to follow the drier ridgelines.

A powerful storm cell overtakes us before we reach solid ground. Lightning flashes across the dark sky as the clouds unload, obscuring the road ahead. If we stop to wait out the storm, we'll be stranded for at least a day until the roads can dry. We press on, pushing our luck, and narrowly avoid getting stuck again and again. At full dark we reach the paved highway—clothes soaked, truck splattered with mud, surprised we made it. The weather forecast had called for clear skies.

A few days later, blue skies stretch between the cliffs of Peach Springs Wash in the western Grand Canyon. My friend Terry Brian, my son Erik, and I drive down the only road that reaches the Colorado River for 280 miles between Lees Ferry and Pearce Ferry. We plan to spend three days running the lower gorge of the Colorado. Having guided river trips since 1971, Terry has lost count of the times he's run the Colorado—at least 150. When not rafting on the Colorado, he leads clients on treks and river expeditions from Tierra del Fuego to Point Barrow. Erik, almost 12 years old, is making his first river trip.

As we descend, the walls take on the classic stepped profile—the cliff-slope-

Spent agave stalk arches to the sky as a rainbow dips into the canyon. Also called the century plant, this member of the amaryllis family takes years to flower, then dies. Agaves long provided a food staple for canyon inhabitants.

bench pattern—that is characteristic of the Grand Canyon. Smoke trees with their pointed, green branches grow on the lower slopes; long, spindly stems of the ocotillo, full-leafed after the recent rains, perch on the higher ledges.

A little past Diamond Creek, the road enters a tight gorge. During a storm, all the runoff from a wide area of the surrounding plateau funnels through the narrows. Frequent floods keep the Hualapai Indians busy maintaining the dirt road.

Terry says that a river company's pickup once got stuck here. A two-ton truck, fully loaded with gear, pulled in behind it to help. Hearing the low-pitched roar of an approaching flash flood, the crews scrambled up a nearby cliff just as a wall of water careened around the bend. Diamond Creek swept both vehicles into the river.

Water in this dry country is an event, dramatic and sometimes violent. It often comes suddenly and is gone as suddenly, draining into rivers entrenched within deep canyons. The cutting force of water has shaped the character of this region on a massive scale. One of the paradoxes of the desert is that it brings you closer to water. You are forced to pay attention to it, to learn its moods.

In 1990 a flash flood tore down Havasu Creek, a tributary of the Colorado River in the Grand Canyon, the home of the Havasupai Indians. A surge of boulders, trees, and silt-thickened water forced those living in the village of Supai to climb the slopes to safety. Their main link with the outside world—a horse and foot trail—washed away.

On the day the storm hit, my friends Ken and Barbara Hodder were on their first hike into Havasu Canyon. They watched the storm clouds, darker than any they had ever seen, fill the sky above the canyon walls. The rain came suddenly, falling in sheets so thick they couldn't see the cliffs 20 feet away. They were on foot, but their four-year-old son was somewhere ahead on horseback with a Havasupai guide.

A great wind whipped the treetops back and forth as Ken and Barbara reached Havasu Creek. Above the roar of the storm they could hear the snap of tree trunks breaking. Torrents of runoff cascaded over the rims of the gorge. Floodwaters quickly funneled together, filling the creek to overflowing.

The couple followed the trail downstream to the footbridge, but found it washed out. Their son and the Indian guide were nowhere in sight. The rising water had cut off Ken and his wife from their child. The creek rose nearly two feet, spreading along the canyon floor, as they stood wondering what to do. A Havasupai woman appeared on the far side of the stream. She stood beneath an umbrella, smiling strangely. "You are going to drown," she shouted at them. "You are all going to die."

A Havasupai man rode up on horseback, telling them to try crossing at a pipeline farther down. But when they got there, it was too late. Propelled by the rushing waters, trees had slammed into the pylons, toppling their last hope of crossing.

By now a tongue of water had cut behind them, leaving them stranded. A Havasupai woman hurrying home told them to follow her. Her house sat on a slight elevation of land where they waited as the flood continued to rise. Soon an old man left the house and to their surprise began wading into the chest-deep water. He calmly felt in front of him with a cane as he headed toward a fast current that could sweep him away. Ken began knotting together garden hoses to use as a rescue line, but the old man soon worked his way to a tree rising above the floodwater. He plucked out a stranded kitten and carried the drenched animal back to the house.

After four hours the water receded enough for the couple to wade across to the village. They found their son safe, and the next day left the canyon by helicopter.

Hearing the first reports of the flood, I decided to hike in and make sure a Havasupai family I knew was safe. The air hung heavy and humid when I reached the creek, hidden behind a screen of willows. The sapling thicket bent downstream, still holding the shape of the moving water that recently had covered it.

The stench of decaying animals buried in piles of driftwood lingered in the air. Horses wandered aimlessly, still stunned by the storm. Only the ravens, scouting the devastation, looked eager for the new day. One sat on the snapped-off trunk of a tree, its folded wings hunching together with each raw call.

Floodwaters had pounded into about a dozen houses near the creek, destroying one, washing another off its foundation, and filling the others with mud and water. The village looked deserted—only a few people moved about in the distance, staying close to their homes.

Terry Uqualla, a fencing-crew supervisor, answered the door of his home when I knocked. He was surprised to see me because he thought no white man had hiked down the trail since the flood. Everyone in the village was getting by, he said, with the National Guard flying in food, blankets, and cots.

After a while I left the village and headed back up the trail. Soon I heard a polite cough behind me and waited as Dale Sinyella caught up. He was leaving the canyon to spend the winter cowboying on a ranch.

As we walked, I asked about the flood. "Lots of water," he said. Dale had been asleep in his rock house on the edge of the village when the flood came. "Water was breaking everything up," he continued. "It was tearing up everything—the fences, the trees. Horses, dogs, and cats got washed away. The whole village was nothing but water. There was water wall to wall."

The danger was too great for him to stay, so he climbed to a high ledge just before the wall of his house washed away. "I didn't want to leave my house," he said. "This is my place, my home."

In 1858, Hualapai Indians guided a military exploring party under the command of Lt. Joseph C. Ives down Diamond Creek into the Grand Canyon. Ives called it the Big Cañon and let it go at that. Sometimes all you can do is stand aside and let a place speak for itself. The expedition returned with the earliest scientific notes on the local geology and the first illustrations of the Grand Canyon. A sketch by expedition artist F. W. von Egloffstein depicts a deep and narrow abyss sunk in perpetual twilight. But von Egloffstein's distorted vision of the Grand Canyon foreshadowed the dark mood of Powell's men when they passed Diamond Creek 11 years later.

Terry, Erik, and I round a curve of the Diamond Creek Road and reach the edge of the river, flowing red. The thick, muddy waters of the Colorado push between the canyon walls, fed by flooding streams higher up.

We park the truck and begin unloading our gear among a crowd of river runners. Many commercial river trips leave the Colorado at this point to avoid crossing a long stretch of flat water below the last rapids. But those who do take out here miss some spectacular sights—the Lower Granite Gorge and the dramatic end of the canyon at the Grand Wash Cliffs. The strong midday sun floods the riverbank as we begin to rig our boat. *(Continued on page 190)*

From around the world, visitors young and old gather in awe at the South Rim's edge. The mile-deep, 277-mile-long gorge attracts nearly five million visitors a year to view a natural wonder that Theodore Roosevelt in 1903 deemed "the one great sight which every American . . . should see."

FOLLOWING PAGES: Chiseled into cliffs at Nankoweap, 800 feet above the Colorado, granaries protected corn for the Anasazi, who farmed in side canyons. Perhaps 2,000 prehistoric sites have come to light, mute testimony to early canyon dwellers. By A.D. 1150, the "ancient ones" had dispersed.

Sinuous, water-carved side canyons, such as Matkatamiba (above), offer intriguing detours for a group of river runners on the Colorado. The once silt-laden river derived its name from the Spanish for "reddish-colored." But, since the completion of Glen Canyon Dam in 1963, much of the silt is captured. Now the river often runs clear blue-green. Tinted brilliant azure by calcium carbonate from a spring upstream, the Little Colorado (opposite) snakes through a precipitous gorge to its confluence with the Colorado.

After loading our river bags into the inflated raft, we climb on board. To add an edge of excitement to the run, we picked a raft about 12 feet long. For the Colorado River, it's a small boat, perhaps too small. Bearded, with his long hair combed back, Terry climbs into the stern and lights a cigar. He'll call the shots. Erik and I wedge ourselves side by side in the bow. Terry gives the youngest boatman some brief paddling instructions. He ends by telling him to stay with the boat if it flips. Erik listens carefully, helped by the sound of the rapid just below.

We paddle the raft into the main current and point the bow downstream. Moving water drops into Diamond Creek Rapid and rolls down a field of broken waves, falling 25 feet in just under half a mile. The speed of the water increases as a wave slaps across the bow, drenching us. With a few powerful strokes, Terry keeps the boat angled into the waves to prevent us from slipping sideways and breaching. The second wave breaks over the tubes in a muddy splash, and the third does the same. "It's cold!" Erik shouts over the surging water.

The waves subside around the first bend, but the current stays strong, whirling and rising in boils. Terry checks his cigar—it's still burning. Erik's hat sits on his head a bit skewed. He takes it off and looks at the muddy splash marks. Suddenly an eddy grabs the raft, pulling down one side and wrenching the paddle from his hand. The power of the river comes as a surprise. Retrieving the paddle, we continue downriver.

A narrow inner gorge of ancient rock channels the water between cliffs sometimes 1,200 feet high. We float on a river that has cut deeply into the Precambrian granite and schist formed nearly two billion years ago. Once the roots of an ancient range of mountains, the metamorphic rock is veined with twisting intrusions. Capped by the level, ordered strata of Paleozoic sedimentary rocks, the old Precambrian rock seems even more dark and chaotic.

Taking the waves head-on, we run the middle of Travertine Rapid and pull in at its foot. Crossing the boulder-studded beach, we enter a slot in the cliff carved through travertine deposits of calcium carbonate. Water, sun warmed and spring fed, splashes down a series of falls. In a deep chamber called Travertine Grotto, a waterfall fills the air with white noise and cool spray. We take turns ducking under the falls and waiting in the shaded canyon until the sun loses its bite.

Later we float downriver to camp next to a high waterfall. A thin stream slides down a graceful travertine curtain, past a hanging garden of maidenhair ferns, clumps of moss, and crimson monkeyflowers. Giant thistles and cattails line the watercourse below. The night is hot and still as we fall asleep.

The sky lightens a shade or two as we roll out the next morning. The craggy walls shape the sky into a ragged band of blue. A lone canyon wren calls in clear, falling notes. After strapping in our river bags, we drift downstream. The color of the water has changed from flash-flood red to coffee brown. As we approach Mile 232 Rapid, Erik wonders if we'll flip. The current slows as we enter the water pooled above the rapid. "The calm before the storm," he predicts, as we

PRECEDING PAGES: Hikers yield the right-of-way to mule-mounted visitors switchbacking along the South Kaibab Trail. "If you fall off," wranglers may tease nervous novices astride the surefooted animals, "the scenery's awful purty on the way down!"

round a shoulder of the cliff. A low rumble comes from ahead. "That sounds big! Really big."

Terry and I once ran the lower gorge with a group of blind people. They showed a degree of self-reliance I hadn't expected—setting up their own camps, washing their dishes. An experienced boatman rowed the first boat through Mile 232, carrying an older woman and a man who could neither see nor hear. The guide set up for a run down the middle, taking a large standing wave straight on. Normally he would have been okay, but the wave broke upstream just as the boat climbed its face. Raft and passengers flipped end over end.

Terry and I reached the capsized boat and fished the swimmers out of the water. To our surprise, the blind woman was smiling. She had been anticipating the trip for two years and had imagined flipping so many times, she would have been disappointed if it hadn't happened. "That was great," she said as we hauled her in.

Reaching the head of Mile 232 Rapid, Terry, Erik, and I pull in to have a look. No one is taking it for granted. We weave through a boulder field of rocks, polished smooth. The force of flowing water has fluted and hollowed them into forms that appear shaped by hand. A debris fan, washed out from a side canyon, constricts the river channel here by half. The current sweeps into a big hole at the top and races through a file of standing waves. But the water is at a forgiving stage, high enough to cover three sharp rocks. Terry points out to Erik the hazards of the run.

We return to the raft and push off, letting the current draw us into the churning water. Erik and I keep paddling as Terry steers from the stern, dodging a hole, tucking the boat behind a breaking wave, and facing into another bow first. The raft leaps skyward and plunges, filling with water. A few moments later, we wash out the bottom of the rapids still right side up.

The river takes us through other rapids and taller waves. Even in the riffles, the boat takes on enough water to keep us bailing. But by afternoon the rough water flattens, and the rapids end before we know it. We keep looking for the last one without realizing we've passed it. The current remains strong, but water from Lake Mead has backed up into the gorge, drowning the remaining rapids.

The three of us float to Separation Canyon, a break in the cliff where Powell's expedition split up. Where there's now only flat water, they ran into a rapid worse than any they had seen. Tremendous waves and rocks filled the channel from wall to wall. Unable to find a way to lower the boats by rope, they had to run it or abandon the river. Three men chose to leave. O. G. and Seneca Howland and William Dunn followed Separation Canyon to its head and climbed out to an uncertain fate. Reports of their deaths at the hands of Paiute Indians reached the Mormon settlements, but their bodies were never recovered. The major and his five remaining men succeeded in running the rapid without loss of life.

Returning to the river after a walk up Separation, I find a string of sharp-prowed dories floating downstream. Trip leader Kenton Grua pulls in to say hello in the boat he built, named the *Grand Canyon*. Lew Steiger parks next to him in the *Black Mesa*. We'll camp with the dories tonight a few miles downriver. They leave an inflatable kayak for one of us to use and continue on to camp with their passengers.

Erik jumps into the inflatable as we pull out. I tell him to stay close since the current is still strong. He circles the raft a few times as we drift downstream, but soon he lets the distance between us widen. I watch his double-bladed paddle flash up and down as he leaves Separation Canyon behind, hurrying to catch the dories. I suppose it always comes as a surprise when a boy strikes out on his own. Terry and I reach camp and land next to the inflatable. Erik stands holding the paddle upright with a big smile on his face, and for the first time he wears his hat turned back.

Passengers spread out across the beach, scurrying to stake claims to the best campsites. The crew doesn't bother—they'll sleep on their boats or close to them. Terry jokes with old friends as they pound stakes in the sand to secure the boats and begin setting up camp. Their experience shows.

Many of the guides have been on the river for 20 years, but their commitment to this place goes beyond the craft of running rivers. Some know the Grand Canyon almost as well off the river as on it. Kenton once left Lees Ferry on foot and ended up at Pearce Ferry 36 days later, having hiked the entire length of the Grand Canyon. All of the crew share a deep connection with the canyon country, a place

that is as much their home as wherever they may live when they're off the river.

After dinner, boatman Pete Gross walks to the river's edge with an alto recorder. Soon the clear notes of Beethoven's "Ode to Joy" drift over the water, amplified by the curve of the canyon wall. The last light fades, and the dark canyon walls stand silhouetted against the lesser dark of the sky. Erik falls asleep on the bottom of an upturned raft, listening to river stories.

Our camp is near the far western edge of the Colorado Plateau. Tomorrow we will leave the Grand Canyon. When Major Powell reached this point in 1869, he was close to filling in one of the last blank spots on the map. But the sense of discovery still remains. Part of it is the tangible research: dinosaur bones and meteorite impact theories, prehistoric roadways and humpback chub. But another part is the feeling that no matter how much we learn, the questions always outrun the answers.

As the canyon country becomes more familiar, the sense of strangeness only deepens. Powell's "Great Unknown" remains just around the next bend of the river.

The next morning Kenton stands in his dory wearing a hat with long earflaps and blowing a conch shell. After breakfast, the passengers leave on a jet boat that comes to take them across the flat water. The crew lashes the baggage boats and dories together into a large raft and mounts a motor for the six-hour trip to Pearce Ferry. We wind through the canyon on water half river and half lake. Walls of faded browns and grays rise beneath a sun turned hazy. We can smell the dust long before we reach the desert beyond. A lone blue heron circles back upriver, its great wings dark against the sky.

The canyon notch widens as we round the final bend, heading west. A mile farther and the cliff walls abruptly end. We pass through the Grand Wash Cliffs,

Maidenhair ferns drape seep-moistened cliffs in Havasu Canyon. Blossoms of beavertail cactus brighten sunbaked slopes along Bass Trail (opposite). For myriad plant communities, the Grand Canyon offers niches from desert to lush glens, from cliffs to sandy beaches.

FOLLOWING PAGES: Sunrise gilds a cliff below Cape Royal as the canyon beyond awaits morning's glow. The cliff's top layers of Kaibab and Toroweap limestone were laid down by ancient seas. The lower layer, of Coconino sandstone, was formed even earlier—when the area was a great desert that covered more than 32,000 square miles.

dropping 3,000 feet from the plateau above. On both sides of us the cliffs give way to the wide light of the desert. The Grand Canyon ends.

For Powell and his men, leaving the Grand Canyon was an escape. They floated away singing and joking. "Now the danger is over," Powell wrote, "now the toil has ceased, now the gloom has disappeared. . . . our joy is almost ecstasy."

But the dory crew is quiet as the Grand Canyon ends and the trip draws to a close. "The first time I left the Grand Wash Cliffs," says boatman Lowell Lundeen, "I was stunned. There were tears in my eyes. The sense of loss is overwhelming— knowing it's ending, that you can't take it with you."

We pass a snowy egret standing stiff-legged against the green of a willow thicket. The Great Basin country stretches before us, and Pearce Ferry will soon be in sight. I look forward to the landing. One trip has to end before the next can begin.

Notes on Photographers

TOM BEAN, a former National Park Service ranger, lives near Flagstaff, Arizona. He has been a steady contributor to National Geographic books, and has photographed for TRAVELER magazine.

A resident of California, **MIGUEL LUIS FAIRBANKS** covered Hells Canyon for TRAVELER, and photographed imperiled Guatemalan forests for NATIONAL GEOGRAPHIC magazine.

DAVID ALAN HARVEY has photographed for the National Geographic in many corners of the world. On his *Canyon Country Parklands* assignment, Dave especially enjoyed working at Colorado's Crow Canyon Archaeological Center. Dave lives in Washington, D.C.

An avid photographer of canyon country, California resident **DEWITT JONES** teaches a photography workshop in the Grand Canyon. Pursuing his work in the American West, Dewitt has published books and contributed to NATIONAL GEOGRAPHIC.

A starry sky, a sliver of moon, the planet Venus, and predawn glow form a backdrop for the Mittens, in Arizona.

Illustrations Credits

FRONT MATTER: 1 Jack W. Dykinga; 2-3 Dewitt Jones; 4-5 Monty Roessel; 6-7 Ric Ergenbright.

GATEWAY: 10-11 Linde Waidhofer/WESTERN EYE; 12 Tom Bean/DRK PHOTO; 14 Ric Ergenbright; 15 Carr Clifton; 17-23 (all) Miguel Luis Fairbanks; 24 (left) Stephen Trimble; 24 (right) George H. H. Huey; 29 Miguel Luis Fairbanks; 30-31 Fred Hirschmann; 32-33 (both) Jack W. Dykinga; 34 Dugald Bremner; 35 Linde Waidhofer/WESTERN EYE; 36-37 Jack W. Dykinga.

THE HIGH PLATEAUS: 38-39 Thomas Wiewandt/WILD HORIZONS; 41 Kerrick James; 42 Rod Planck/TOM STACK & ASSOCIATES; 43 Dewitt Jones; 44-45 Fred Hirschmann; 46-47 Dugald Bremner; 47 William Ervin/COMSTOCK INC.; 48-49 Steven Mangold/WESTLIGHT; 53-54 (both) Dewitt Jones; 56 Coby Jordan; 57 Zandria Muench; 58-59 Floyd Holdman; 62 Bruce Hucko; 63 Jack Olson; 64-65 Eugene Fisher.

WILDLIFE OF THE GREAT PLATEAU: 66-67 George F. Mobley, National Geographic Photographer; 68-69 Thomas Wiewandt/WILD HORIZONS; 69 Fred Hirschmann; 70 (upper) EARTH SCENES/Mickey Gibson; 70 (lower) David Hiser/PHOTOGRAPHERS ASPEN; 70-71 (upper) Ric Ergenbright; 70-71 (lower) EARTH SCENES/Fred Whitehead; 71 Floyd Holdman; 72 ANIMALS ANIMALS/Zig Leszczynski; 72-73 Michael H. Francis; 73 (upper) Steve Howe/THIRD PLANET; 73 (center) Michael H. Francis; 73 (lower) Dewitt Jones; 74 (upper and center) Robert F. Sisson; 74 (lower) Dewitt Jones; 75 Stephen Trimble; 76 (upper) William E. Ferguson; 76 (lower) Thomas Wiewandt/WILD HORIZONS; 76-77 Bruce Dale, National Geographic Photographer; 78-79 Thomas Wiewandt/WILD HORIZONS; 79 (upper) Scott T. Smith; 79 (lower) D. Robert Franz/THE WILDLIFE COLLECTION; 80-81 Wayne Lankinen/DRK PHOTO.

HEARTLANDS: 82-83 Linde Waidhofer/WESTERN EYE; 84 Dugald Bremner; 86 Salvatore Vasapolli; 87-89 (both) Jack W. Dykinga; 90 Scott T. Smith; 93 David Hiser; 94 Scott S. Warren; 94-95 David Hiser/PHOTOGRAPHERS ASPEN; 96-97 David Muench; 98-99 David Alan Harvey; 100-101 Art Wolfe; 101 Scott Sroka; 102-103 Dewitt Jones; 106 Michael Norton/ADSTOCK PHOTOS; 109 Dewitt Jones; 110-111 Greg Lashbrook/F-STOCK, INC.; 112-113 Gary Ladd; 115 Carr Clifton; 117 Stephen Trimble; 118-119 Dewitt Jones; 119 (upper) Stephen Trimble; 119 (lower)-123 (all) Dewitt Jones; 124-125 Marc Muench.

PEOPLE OF THE GREAT PLATEAU: 126-127 Robert Winslow/TOM STACK & ASSOCIATES; 128 David Alan Harvey; 131 Stephen Trimble; 132-133 Eugene Fisher; 134 Stephen Trimble; 134-139 (all) David Alan Harvey; 140 Stephen Trimble; 141 Eugene Fisher; 144 (upper) Jerry Jacka; 144 (lower) Stephen Trimble; 144-145 Stephen Trimble; 146 John Running; 150-153 (all) Ira Block; 154-155 George H. H. Huey; 155 David Alan Harvey; 156 Fred Hirschmann; 157 George H. H. Huey; 159 Phil Schofield; 160 David Hiser/PHOTOGRAPHERS ASPEN; 161 Michael S. Sample; 162-163 (both) David Alan Harvey; 164-165 Paul Chesley/PHOTOGRAPHERS ASPEN; 165 George H. H. Huey; 166-167 Bob Sacha.

GRAND CANYON MAJESTY: 168-169 Jim Brandenburg/MINDEN PICTURES; 171 Tom Bean; 172 Dugald Bremner; 173 Tom Bean; 174-175 Jack W. Dykinga; 176-177 (both) Thomas Wiewandt/WILD HORIZONS; 178 David Edwards; 182-183 (both) Miguel Luis Fairbanks; 184-185 Fred Hirschmann; 186 David Edwards; 187 Tom Bean; 188-189 David Hiser/PHOTOGRAPHERS ASPEN; 192 Larry Ulrich; 193 Thomas Wiewandt/WILD HORIZONS; 194-195 Larry Ulrich.

BACK MATTER: 196 Kerrick James.

Index

Boldface indicates illustrations.

Agaves **70, 71, 178,** 179
Agenbroad, Larry 108, 114
Anasazi Indians: dwellings and house sites 129-130, 143, 147, 149, vandalism of 114; farming 183; migrations 60, 142, 143, 148
Anderson, Bruce 149
Arches **82-83, 86, 96-97;** collapse 104-105; formation 85
Arches NP, Utah 200; formations **82-83, 86, 87, 88,** 104-105; juniper tree **86**
Aspen trees **78-79**
Aztec Ruins NM, N. Mex. 142; restored great kiva **165**

Balanced Rock, Arches NP, Utah **88-89**
Bandelier NM, N. Mex.: cliff dwelling **161**
Beavertail cactus **192**
Behind the Rocks country, near Canyonlands NP, Utah **93**
Behunin family cabin, Capitol Reef NP, Utah **118-119**
Belnap, Jayne 92
Bradley, Bruce 143
Bristlecone pine **43**
Brown, Barnum 28
Bryce, Ebenezer 43
Bryce Canyon NP, Utah 43, 50-52, 200; formations **42, 44-45,** 47, **48-49;** ski trail **46-47**
Buffalo dance **152-153**
Buttes **6-7**

Camptosaurus 26
Canyon de Chelly NM, Ariz. 149
Canyonlands NP, Utah **100-101,** 200; crater 104; formations **90, 96-97;** maze country 86-87, 91-92; opera performance **94;** tourism 107; trails **94-95,** 105; valley formation 106
Cape Royal: cliff below **194-195**
Capitol Reef NP, Utah 200; crystals **122;** formations **115,** 107-108, 114, **123, 124-125**
Carleton, James 158
Carson, Kit 158

Casa Rinconada, Chaco Canyon, N. Mex. 140, 165, **166-167**
Cassidy, Butch 50
Cataract Canyon, Canyonlands NP, Utah **90**
Cathedral Rock, Ariz. **12**
Cedar Breaks NM, Utah 40, **41**
Chaco Canyon, N. Mex. 140, 141-142
Chaco Culture NHP, N. Mex.: New Age ceremonies 140; village ruins **164-165**
Chamberlain, Von Del 160-161
Chub, humpback: protection studies 173
Chure, Dan 26, 27
Cliff Palace, Mesa Verde NP, Colo. 143
Colleran, Jim 143, 147
Colorado Plateau 13; climate 68, 69; formation 16, 24, 68, 69; map 8-9
Colorado River, U. S.-Mexico **112-113,** 172, 186
Concha belts **134,** 135
Coronado, Francisco Vásquez de 131
Cottonwood trees **15, 119**
Cowboys: herding cattle **159**
Coyote **73**
Coyote (Paiute legend) 42
Crow Canyon Archaeological Center, Colo.: study group **162-163**
Cryptobiotic soil 92

Davenport, Marietta 147-148
Deertrap Mountain, Zion NP, Utah 52
Deluge Shelter, Dinosaur NM, Colo.-Utah 25; pictographs **29**
Desert bighorn sheep **72**
Desert cottontail **72**
Desert spiny lizard **73**
Devils Garden, Arches NP, Utah **86**
Dimock, Brad 14, 15, 16, 21, 24, 25
Dinosaur fossils **23;** bones 26, 27, 28-29; embryo 26; footprints **24,** 28
Dinosaur NM, Colo.-Utah **17,** 25, 29; fossil excavations **22-23,** 26, 27
Dinosaur Quarry, Dinosaur NM, Colo.-Utah 26
Dirty Devil Canyon, Dirty Devil River, Utah **110-111**
The Doll House, Canyonlands NP, Utah **90,** 105
Douglas firs **47**
Dugout Ranch, near Canyonlands NP, Utah **98-99,** 106-107

Eaton, Jeff 51
Echo Park, Dinosaur NM, Colo.-Utah **17,** 25
Elder, Ann **22, 23,** 27

Fancy dancer **128**
Fish, Joseph 43
Ford, Dabney 131, 140-141
Fossils: dinosaur **23, 24,** 26, 27, 28-29; petrified wood 27, **32-33**
Fremont Indians 108; headdresses 25; pictographs **29**

Glass Mountain, Capitol Reef NP, Utah **122**
Glen Canyon Dam, Ariz. 104, 113, 116-117, 186
Glen Canyon NRA, Utah-Ariz. **2-3,** 107, 108, **112-113,** 113, 114, 116-117; vandalism 114
The Grabens, Canyonlands NP, Utah 106
Grand Canyon NP, Ariz. 168-195, 200
Grand Falls, Little Colorado River, Ariz. **173**
Green River, U. S. **17,** 26 rapids **20-21,** 29
Gunnison River, Colo. **15**
Gustafson, Terry 85-87, 91-92, 104-108, 114

Hackberry trees 78, **79**
Havasu Canyon, Ariz.: flash flood 180-181
Havasu Creek, Ariz. **172, 176-177**
Havasupai Indians 177, 180
Hedgehog cactus **76**
Honey ants **76-77**
Hoodoos **42,** 43, **44-45,** 52
Hopi Indians 129, **144-145, 146;** corn 144-145; migrations 130; rites 14, 129, 130
Horsetail plants **24, 70-71**
House finches **74**
Hualapai Indians 180, 181
Hubbell, John Lorenzo 155, 156, 157
Hubbell Trading Post NHS, Ganado, Ariz. **154-155,** 156-157
Hudec, Mike 104
Hunter, Wilson 158, 160

Isis Temple, Grand Canyon NP, Ariz. 173, **175**
Island in the Sky mesa, Canyonlands NP, Utah: arch **96-97;** opera performance **94;** trail **94-95**
Ives, Joseph C. 181

Jacobs, Chris 52, **53**
Jake, Clifford 60, 61, 62-63
Joblove, Rod **22,** 27
Johnson, Bill 158
Juniper tree **70-71**

Kachinas 129; dances 130; dolls
  144, 145
Keet Seel, Navajo NM, Ariz. 147-
  148
Kinaalda (Navajo ceremony) 4
Kolob Arch, Zion NP, Utah 105
Kolob Canyons, Utah 60-61
Kopf, Rudi 104

La Sal Mountains, Utah **93;**
  avalanche 51
Landscape Arch, Arches NP, Utah:
  collapse 104-105
Last Chance Bay, Utah **109**
Lee, John D. 61
Legend People 42
Leslie, Delfred 130, 131
Leslie, Ebin 130
Little Colorado River, Ariz. 172, **173,**
  186, **187**
Lower Cathedral Valley, Capitol
  Reef NP, Utah **115;** crystals
  122

McKnight, Frank 26
Madsen, Scott **23,** 26-27, 28, 29
Maidenhair ferns **58-59, 193**
Malone, Bill and Minnie **155,** 157
Mammoths: petroglyphs 108;
  remains 108, 114
Manzanita 50
Mariposa lily **117**
Mason, Charlie 143
Massacre Cave, Canyon de Chelly
  NM, Ariz. 157-158
Mather Point, Grand Canyon NP,
  Ariz.: view from **174-175**
Matkatamiba Canyon, Grand Canyon
  NP, Ariz. **186**
May, Tommy 147
The Maze, Canyonlands NP, Utah 86-
  87, 91-92
Medicine men 141
Mesa Arch, Canyonlands NP, Utah
  96-97
Mesa Verde NP, Colo. 142-143, 200
Mittens (buttes), Monument Valley,
  Utah-Ariz. **6, 196**
Moenave formation, Painted Desert,
  Ariz. 28-29
Monument Basin, Canyonlands NP,
  Utah **100-101**

Monument Valley, Utah-Ariz. **6-7,**
  68-69
Moore, Lige 50
Mormons: Kolob escape trail 61;
  militia 61; settlement in Utah 43,
  61, **118-119**
Morris, Earl 142, 149, 156
Morrison formation, Dinosaur NM,
  Colo.-Utah 26, 27
Mountain lion **66-67**
Mountain Meadows, Utah: massacre
  (1857) 61
Muir, John: on Grand Canyon 170
Mule deer 78, **79**
Mummy Cave, Canyon de Chelly NM,
  Ariz.: excavation 156

Nankoweap Creek, Grand Canyon
  NP, Ariz.: granaries **185**
The Narrows, Virgin River, Utah 56,
  57; rockfall 61
Navajo Indians **5,** 160; dancers
  134-135; defeat at Canyon
  de Chelly 158; folklore 42, 68,
  141, 149; hogan 131, **133;**
  livestock **136-137;** pottery **131;**
  rites 4, 14; rugs **154-155;** star
  ceilings 161
Navajo Loop Trail, Bryce Canyon NP,
  Utah **46-47**
Navajo Mountain, Utah 52
Neboyia, Chauncey **141,** 149, 161
The Needles, Canyonlands NP, Utah:
  vehicle traffic 107
Newspaper Rock HM, Utah:
  petroglyphs **101**
North Creek, Zion NP, Utah **56**

Oak Creek, Ariz. **12**
The Organ, Arches NP, Utah **87**
Othole, Andrew 131
Ott, Wallace 43, 50, 52

Padre Bay, Glenn Canyon NRA, Utah
  2-3
Painted Desert, Ariz. **24,** 27, 28;
  fossil excavations 28, 29;
  petroglyph panel **29**
Painted Desert Inn, Petrified Forest
  NP, Ariz. 27
Paiute Indians 42, 43, 60, 191, 192
Paria Canyon-Vermilion Cliffs
  Wilderness Area, Utah **1, 34, 35,**
  36-37
Paunsaugunt Plateau: erosion 42-43,
  50; hoodoo **42**
Petrified Forest NP, Ariz. 27, **32-33,**
  200

Petrified wood 27, **32-33**
Petroglyphs **30-31, 101;** mammoth
  depiction 108
Pictographs **29,** 87
Pink Cliffs, Utah 42, 51
Pipe Spring NM, Ariz. 156, **157**
Ponderosa pines **69**
Potholes **54,** 69, 74, **75**
Powell, John Wesley 13-14, 25, 26,
  43, 60, 104, 170, 173, 193; "Great
  Unknown" 172; survey 122
Powell, Lake, Utah **109;** kayakers
  110-111; marina **102-103;** water-
  skier **106**
Powwows **128,** 129, **134-135**
Pratt, Parley P. 61
Prickly pear cactuses **70**
Protosuchus 29
Pueblo Alto, Chaco Canyon, N. Mex.
  140, 141
Pueblo Bonito, Chaco Culture NHP,
  N. Mex. 141, **164-165**
Pueblo Indians: adobe oven **151;**
  dances 151, **152-153;** dwelling
  151; elder **150;** engineering
  accomplishments 131, 141; great
  kivas 140

Quilt, Double Wedding Ring **156**

Rattlesnake **74**
Redd, Hardy 158
Redd, Heidi **98,** 106, 107
Roosevelt, Theodore: on Grand
  Canyon 183
Rufous hummingbird **80-81**

Sacred datura **14**
Sand Canyon Pueblo, near Mesa
  Verde NP, Colo. 143
Sandstone **1, 12, 34, 35, 38-39,**
  43, 46-47; Cedar Mesa 104,
  107; Coconino 193; Entrada
  84, 104, **115;** Kaibab 193;
  Kayenta **56;** Moenave 28; Navajo
  10-11, 28, 54-55, **109,** 114;
  Toroweap 193; water permeation
  62, 63; White Rim **100-101;**
  Wingate 106, 114; *see also*
  Arches; Buttes; Hoodoos;
  Potholes
Shafer Trail Road, Canyonlands
  NP, Utah: mountain bikers
  94-95
Shoemaker, Gene 104
Sinyella, Dale 181
Sleight, Ken 116-117
South Kaibab Trail, Grand Canyon

NP, Ariz. **188-189**
South Rim, Grand Canyon NP, Ariz.:
view from **182-183**
Spider Rock, Canyon de Chelly NM, Ariz. 136, **138-139,** 149
Spider Woman (Navajo legend) 141, 149
Spirit Seep, Zion NP, Utah **62**
Split Mountain, Dinosaur NM, Colo.-Utah 26
Spotted owl **73**
Spruce Tree House, Mesa Verde NP, Colo. **126-127,** 129
Steamboat Rock, Dinosaur NM, Colo.-Utah **17**
Sunset Crater Volcano NM, Ariz. **160**

Tadpole shrimp **74**
Taos Pueblo, N. Mex. **151**
Temple of the Sun, Capitol Reef NP, Utah **115**
Thor's Hammer, Bryce Canyon NP, Utah 43, **44-45**
Thybony, Scott **23**
Tiger Wall, Yampa River, Colo. 16, **18-19**
Tower House, Canyon de Chelly NM, Ariz. 156
Trees for Mother Earth 158
Tropic, Utah 43
Tucupit Point 60
Turret Arch, Arches NP, Utah **82-83**

Upheaval Dome, Canyonlands NP, Utah 104
Uqualla, Terry 181
Ute Indians 147
Ute Mountain Tribal Park, Colo. 147

Virgin River, Utah 56, **57**
Vivian, Gwinn 142

Wahweap marina, Ariz. **102-103**
Watchman's sandstone, Zion NP, Utah **64-65**
Waterpocket Fold, Capitol Reef NP, Utah 107-108, 114, **123, 124-125**
Weeping Rock, Zion NP, Utah 63
West Temple, Zion NP, Utah **38-39,** 40
Wetherill, John 147-148
Wetherill, Richard 143, 147
White Rim, Monument Basin, Canyonlands NP, Utah **100-101**
Whitla, Russell 148

Williams, Tony 52, 54, 55, 61, 63, 85-87, 91-92, 104-107
Wilson, David 158
Window Rock, Ariz. 135
The Windows, Arches NP, Utah: arch **82-83**
Winsor Castle, Pipe Spring NM, Ariz.: parlor 156, **157**

Yaki Point, Grand Canyon NP, Ariz.:
view from **168-169**
Yampa River, Colo. 14-15, 16, **17, 18-19, 20-21,** 25; flash flood (1965) 24

Zion NP, Utah 200; formations **38-39,** 52, **64-65;** rivers **57;** rockfall 61; sandstone climbing 55; trails 63
Zuni Indians 131

Acknowledgments

The Book Division wishes to thank the individuals, groups, and organizations named or quoted in the text. We are especially grateful for the assistance given us by George H. Billingsley, Stephen Trimble, and the superintendents and staff of the National Park System. We would also like to thank Eirik A.T. Blom, Greer Chesher, Jane Cole, Terri Green, Maggie Magee, Keela Mangum, Lora Rasmussen, David Whitman, William Xanton, and Phil Zichterman.

Additional Reading

The reader may wish to consult the *National Geographic Index* for related articles and books, in particular *National Geographic's Guide to the National Parks of the United States.* National Park Service Handbooks and the KC Publications park series *The Story Behind the Scenery* may also be of interest, as well as the following books: Edward Abbey, *Desert Solitaire;* Edward Abbey and Philip Hyde, *Slickrock: The Canyon Country of Southeast Utah;* Donald L. Baars, *The Colorado Plateau: A Geologic History;* C. Gregory Crampton, *Land of Living Rock* and *Standing Up Country;* Natt Dodge, *Flowers of the Southwest Deserts;* W. Kenneth Hamblin and Joseph R. Murphy, *Grand Canyon Perspectives;* David V. Harris and Eugene P. Kiver, *The Geologic Story of the National Parks and Monuments;* J. Donald Hughes, *In the House of Stone and Light;* Dewitt Jones and Stephen Trimble, *Canyon Country;* Robert H. and Florence C. Lister, *Those Who Came Before;* John Wesley Powell, *The Exploration of the Colorado River and Its Canyons;* Stephen Trimble, *The Bright Edge: A Guide to the National Parks of the Colorado Plateau;* Ann Zwinger, *Run, River, Run.*

Library of Congress CIP Data
Thybony, Scott.
    Canyon country parklands : treasures of the Great Plateau / by Scott Thybony ;
prepared by the Book Division, National Geographic Society.
     p. cm.
    Includes index.
    ISBN 0-87044-907-9
    1. National parks and reserves--Colorado Plateau.   I. National Geographic
Society (U.S.). Book Division. II. Title.
F788.T5   1993
979.1'3--dc20   93-3517
                                                 CIP

Composition for this book by the Typographic section of National Geographic Production Services, Pre-Press Division. Set in Cheltenham Book. Printed and bound by R. R. Donnelley & Sons, Willard, Ohio. Color separations by Graphic Art Service, Inc., Nashville, Tenn.; Lanman Progressive Co., Washington, D.C.; Lincoln Graphics, Inc., Cherry Hill, N.J.; and Phototype Color Graphics, Pennsauken, N.J. Dust jacket printed by Miken Inc., Cheektowaga, N.Y.

THE NATIONAL PARKS OF CANYON COUNTRY

☆ **Arches NP, P.O. Box 907, Moab, Utah 84532, (801) 259-8161**   *Highlights:* Numerous sandstone arches including Delicate Arch, Courthouse Towers, Windows, Fiery Furnace, Balanced Rock, Devils Garden, fins, spires, pinnacles, and slickrock.   *Activities:* Nature hikes, geological and historical exhibits, jeep tours, horseback trail rides, hiking.   *Information:* Visitor Center at main entrance. One campground; 7-day limit. Permits are required for backcountry camping. Summer temperatures can reach 110°F. Hikers must carry water and stay on trails—cryptobiotic crust is fragile and takes years to recover. Slickrock crumbles easily and can make climbing extremely dangerous. Some unpaved roads may become impassable after heavy rains.

☆ **Bryce Canyon NP, Utah 84717, (801) 834-5322**   *Highlights:* Pink Cliffs, Thor's Hammer, Bryce Canyon 18 miles long, up to 5 miles wide, hoodoos, amphitheaters, pinnacles.   *Activities:* Hiking and horseback riding, prairie dog and other nature walks, history and geology talks, exhibits, night sky programs, moonlight walks, cross-country skiing, snowshoeing.   *Information:* Visitor Center on main road one mile inside the park. Two campgrounds; 14-day limit. Hikers must carry water. Permits are required for backcountry camping; allowed only on Under-the-Rim Trail. Watch children at all times; falls can be fatal. High elevation is dangerous for those with heart or respiratory problems. Roads closed during and immediately after snowstorms.

☆ **Canyonlands NP, 125 W. 200 South, Moab, Utah 84532, (801) 259-7164**   *Highlights:* The Needles, The Maze, Island in the Sky, pinnacles, arches, fins, pictographs. *Activities:* Hiking, rafting, canoeing, kayaking, mountain biking. Also, four-wheel-drive, mountain-biking, hiking, river-running trips offered by concessionaires. *Information:* Visitor Centers just inside entrances to Island in the Sky and The Needles and at the Hans Flat Ranger Station just outside the park in Glen Canyon NRA. Two campgrounds; 7-day limit. Permits are required for backcountry camping. Do not walk on cryptobiotic crust. Use caution near cliff edges and on slickrock; falls can be fatal. Always carry water. Flash floods from July to September can temporarily close some roads.

☆ **Capitol Reef NP, Torrey, Utah 84775, (801) 425-3791**   *Highlights:* 100-mile-long Waterpocket Fold, historical district of Fruita, Cathedral Valley, Chimney Rock.   *Activities:* Nature walks, hiking, fruit picking, bird-watching, guided horseback trips, jeep tours.   *Information:* Visitor Center at north end of park near Fruita. Three campgrounds; 14-day limit. Permits are required for backcountry camping. Always carry water. Watch out for flash floods throughout summer season. Back roads can become impassable during spring thaw, summer rains, and winter snows at higher elevations.

☆ **Grand Canyon NP, P.O. Box 129, Grand Canyon, Arizona 86023, (602) 638-7888**   *Highlights:* Mile-deep, 277-mile-long gorge cut by the Colorado River; exposed rock at the canyon floor, 1.7 billion years old. *Activities:* Day and evening nature walks, campfire programs, horse and mule trips into the canyon, hiking, bicycling, fishing, river rafting, sight-seeing flights, cross-country skiing.   *Information:* Visitor Center on the South Rim in Grand Canyon Village and information on the North Rim in Grand Canyon Lodge. Four campgrounds; 7-day limit. Permits are required for backcountry camping. Be very careful near the rim; protective barriers are intermittent. North Rim is closed from late October to mid-May because of deep snow.

☆ **Mesa Verde NP, Colorado 81330, (303) 529-4465**   *Highlights:* Cliff Palace, Wetherill Mesa, Long House, Balcony House, Spruce Tree House; more than 4,000 prehistoric sites, including Anasazi cliff dwellings, dating from about A.D. 550 to 1270.   *Activities:* Archaeological walks, tours of ruins, wayside exhibits, evening campfire programs, bicycling, limited hiking. Also cross-country skiing and snowshoeing.   *Information:* Visitor Center at Far View in north end of park, open only in summer. Chapin Mesa Museum at south end of park open year-round. One campground; 7-day limit. Backcountry camping not permitted in park. Visits to cliff dwellings are strenuous and not for those with heart or respiratory problems. Hold on to your children on cliff trails and canyon rims. Many services and some roads closed in winter.

☆ **Petrified Forest NP, Arizona 86028, (602) 524-6228**   *Highlights:* Painted Desert, Rainbow Forest, Newspaper Rock, Anasazi ruins and petroglyphs, largest concentration of petrified wood in the world, badlands, plant and animal fossils.   *Activities:* Nature talks, film, hiking.   *Information:* Painted Desert Visitor Center at north entrance. Rainbow Forest Museum near south entrance. No campgrounds in park. Permits are required for backcountry camping. It is illegal to remove rocks, plants, animals, or artifacts from this or any other national park. Stay on trails to prevent damage to desert environment and to avoid being cut on sharp rocks. Always carry water. Do not approach wildlife; animals may carry bubonic plague. Snow and ice may close park road temporarily in winter.

☆ **Zion NP, Springdale, Utah 84767, (801) 772-3256**   *Highlights:* Great White Throne, Watchman, Great Arch, 3,000-foot sandstone cliffs, slickrock, hanging valleys.   *Activities:* Nature walks and talks, evening programs, children's activities, hiking, horseback trail rides, tram tours, climbing, bicycling, river tubing, cross-country skiing.   *Information:* Zion Canyon Visitor Center at South Entrance and Kolob Canyons Visitor Center in northwest corner of park. Three campgrounds; 14-day limit. Permits are required for backcountry camping. Summer temperatures can exceed 105°F. Always carry water. Watch out for rattlesnakes. Dirt roads are impassable when wet. Some roads are closed in winter.